Invest In Your Debt!

How to get a 37.13% guaranteed, risk-free tax-free return* on your investment by first eliminating your debt

*Typical Spend Smart Family

**Dave Ireland, Dave Leuthold, Keith Phildius and Greg Frank
As told to Bill Keenan**

Fourth Edition
Basil A. Watson
Invest In Your Debt
P.O. Box 2241
Danbury, CT 06813-2241
Tel.#203-778-2991

Invest In Your Debt!

Fourth Edition
©Copyright 2001, 2005, 2007 Bill Keenan All Rights Reserved

Sixth Printing 2007

ISBN 0-9713073-0-X

Printed by IYD Inc.
888-913-8786

Table of Contents

Chapter One

Invest in Your Debt

There is a great financial opportunity out there, and it is just for YOU, and it is right at your doorstep. You are interested in financial opportunity, aren't you?

If you are like many people out there you probably have been thinking that you have missed out on financial opportunity altogether or that you wouldn't know where to begin to look for even one such opportunity. You may have thought that even if you did find such an opportunity, it would be wasted because you don't have the time, money or knowledge to make a go of it.

Many people feel they missed an opportunity with the tremendous stock market growth over the last number of years. Many people made a lot of money on that growth, and many people lost a lot of money at the same time. And, for sure, many more felt that "if only this or if only that" they too could have reaped some great rewards from that bull market. Did you get "your share" of that stock market growth or do you feel like that bull market passed you by and just benefited everyone else? Either way, relax. Financial opportunity is still within your grasp.

We call our book and our class *Invest in Your Debt* because it teaches you how to build real wealth and achieve true financial freedom by treating your debt as an investment. An investment is nothing more than a financial opportunity and the purpose of this book is to show you…

<u>Your debt is actually a financial opportunity waiting to happen!</u>

Now you are probably thinking we must be crazy to say debt is an opportunity. Most people look at debt as a burden with seemingly never-ending monthly payments. While we agree that for most people debt is a burden that can destroy future wealth, your debt can actually be turned into a financial opportunity **if** you make the right decisions and choices. *Invest in Your Debt* is all about choices and changing our perceptions in order to achieve true financial freedom.

How on earth, can debt be an opportunity you ask? Consider your debt…how much money do you have going out the door each month for car payments, credit card payments, mortgage payments, debt consolidation loans, home equity loans, student loans and other credit payments?
Is it $500? $1000? Do you spend $2000, $3000 or more, each month on "payments?" We see people in our classes spending $5000 or more on debt each month! As you'll learn later in this book, the sad thing is people are giving away their future wealth and they don't even realize it because they are just using "smart money" as conventional wisdom says.

***Invest in Your Debt* is your opportunity to RECLAIM the money currently going out the door to make your debt payments!**

Think about that concept, "reclaiming" the money you are currently wasting on debt. Why do we use the word "reclaim?" Because you give up your claim to the money in interest and payments, you sent the creditors when you buy something on credit. Investing in your debt will allow you to say to your creditors "I decided to keep this money for myself and my family."

The opportunity of IYD is to take the money you've been giving to your creditors and find a better use for it.

This is your opportunity to put this money back in your pocket! What would your life be like if you could take the money you've been sending to your creditors and use it for something else? What else might you be doing? Where else might you be going? Who else might you be helping? If you had no debt payments, how would you be doing on your current income? You can build your motivation to follow IYD when you ask yourself these questions.

Most people have some debt payments, at least a few hundred dollars a month, so the IYD program applies to almost everyone. If you can eliminate your debt, quickly, then you would have $500, $1000, maybe even $2000 or more "extra" each month. With that extra money, couldn't you then begin to do something better with it? Maybe you could begin building real wealth and achieving true financial freedom.

The typical family actually has debt payments of a little less than $2000 each month. Now if your monthly debt payments are $2000 or more, don't feel **too** bad. This just means you have a BIGGER OPPORTUNITY. Yes, it might take more time (or it might take less time) to eliminate your debt, but when you do, you will have more money available each month to use towards your financial freedom! This will make more sense as you read on.

Don't get us wrong on this "bigger opportunity" concept, however. If your payments are only a few hundred dollars a month, we don't want you running out and buying a new car or maxing out your credit cards, **just so you can have a bigger opportunity!**

The *Invest in Your Debt* program is a completely new strategy. Have you ever heard Paul Harvey on the radio? He tells fascinating stories known as "The Rest of the Story." Think of this book as "the rest of the story" regarding your financial life. We are absolutely convinced that once you know "the rest of the story," and realize the opportunity that lies ahead, you will make the decision to begin your personal journey to true financial freedom using these life-changing concepts and strategies.

Other Financial Strategies

So what about the traditional or typical financial strategies you have heard about all of your lives? You've heard the cliché called "conventional wisdom." Most people approach their financial lives by following conventional wisdom. Conventional wisdom is usually thought of as "what the smart people say."

What is some of the popular conventional wisdom in the financial arena? Have you ever heard some of these?

- Pay yourself first!
- Build a six-month safety net of cash.
- Your house is your biggest asset.
- Don't pay off your mortgage – it's the last tax shelter you have left!

- Credit cards are financial tools because you can use someone else's money for a month.
- You need to invest any extra money you have in your 401K, IRA, mutual funds, etc.

Unfortunately, conventional wisdom in the financial arena often comes from people with a stake, or a reason, for getting you to see things their way. Often their "wisdom" is shaped by the fact that they want you to buy their products (insurance, investments, real estate, etc.). Not that these people are bad, but their advice is biased. So at the very least, it should not be accepted without question. Conventional Wisdom will not help most people achieve **TRUE** financial freedom.

From the perspective of Conventional Wisdom, Financial Freedom today is defined as "Keeping up with the Joneses." Having the big $600,000 house up on the hill (with a $750,000 mortgage because it's cheap money!). Leasing both cars so you can drive "more car for the money." Belonging to the best country club and sending your children to the best private school. Having everything you could possibly want and GETTING IT NOW because you need instant gratification.

We are not saying there is something wrong with having these dreams and aspirations for our children and ourselves. In a free country, life is about choices as it should be. However, don't confuse true financial freedom with the type of life described above, where you give away your future wealth in order to feed your need for instant gratification.

Years of exposure to advertising have shaped our picture of financial freedom. From the "Madison Avenue" perspective, we have come to believe that we can have any and everything whenever we want it if we just use credit to get it. The promise of debt is that it will allow us to have the good life now. **The irony of this promise is that in order to have everything we want now, we have to promise our future wealth to our creditors.**

The idea behind credit is how you can get what you want if you don't have enough cash for the purchase, but you do have enough cash so that you can make "low monthly payments." That way you can fill your need for instant gratification now! Of course, over the future you will make many monthly payments and pay three or four or 10 or 20 times more when you buy something with credit rather than buy something with cash.

Thanks to the truth in lending laws passed in the 1970s, the mortgage companies now tell you that a house you buy for $100,000 will really cost you $300,000 in payments spread out over 30 years. However, the same laws don't require the credit card companies to tell you that the $2000 sofa you just bought will cost you $10,000 in payments if you pay only the minimum monthly payment.

True financial freedom can never be achieved by paying 3 or 4 or 10 or 20 times more than you need to.

Madison Avenue's version of financial freedom is one where you buy a lot of stuff, usually on credit, because you must have it now!

True Financial Freedom is about owning not buying. And, it's not about just owning "stuff." **True Financial Freedom is achieved when you own your life, your time and your future!**

For most of us today, money is often the most important consideration when making decisions. This happens because we are close to the limit on our monthly budgets where we have as much money going out each month as we have coming in. Now, we are not saying money should not be considered when making decisions. However, if you could eliminate one of your largest expenses, so that you have "extra" money each month, that would probably influence your financial decisions, wouldn't it?

As you will see in this book, debt is the largest expense for most people.

Unless you rid yourself of your largest expense (debt payments), you probably will not achieve True Financial Freedom!

The IYD process will teach you how to eliminate all debt. You will learn how to get rid of all your consumer debt (credit cards, car payments, student loans, etc.) in one to three years and then get rid of your 30-year mortgage in another four to five years. You will see you can do this on the income you make today; you don't need a second job, you don't need to live like a hermit in the Himalayas. With the IYD process, you get to have fun and enjoy life while you invest in your debt.

So conventional wisdom says financial freedom is about buying stuff. It goes without saying that there is nothing wrong with buying things. But, when you buy on credit, you will be able to buy much less over a lifetime because of the additional costs of credit. We know from experience that true financial freedom is about owning your life. You will see throughout this book many instances where we compare conventional wisdom to IYD. It is important to study these contrasts to better understand what you can do to stay on track for your goals while avoiding the detours and dead ends of credit and debt.

We take a different perspective with our IYD process. We say…

- Pay your banker first (usually all the bankers stand and cheer when they hear this)
- If you don't have a six-month safety net by now, forget about the safety net until you are debt free
- Your house is your biggest liability (until you pay it off!)
- The mortgage tax deduction is the worst reason in the world to keep your mortgage
- Credit cards always cost you more than cash
- The first step in investing is to invest any extra money you have in your debt!
- Once debt has been eliminated, then invest any extra money you have in your 401K, IRA, mutual funds, etc.

You can see that *Invest in Your Debt* is a very different approach to your financial situation than conventional wisdom. We believe conventional wisdom, especially about debt, needs to be changed. Consumer debt is still a relatively new phenomenon of the last 40 years. We only now have the second generation of credit users hitting the market. Conventional wisdom has not considered consumer debt.

Our grandparents didn't have credit cards. They bought their "stuff" with cash. If they didn't have the cash, they waited and saved until they did! (Remember layaway?) They usually didn't even have a mortgage, or if they did, it was for five years or less. Yet today our kids graduate from high school and college not knowing that credit cards aren't "free money." They don't realize that making minimum payments can stretch your payments out 30 years or more.

How is *Invest in Your Debt* Different?

So, is *Invest in Your Debt* just about paying off debt? What's so new or different about that? As you may know, there are dozens of books about "managing" or even "eliminating your debt." Maybe you've even been to a class or a seminar that teaches the benefits of debt freedom. As you start reading this text, it is important that you understand how…

Invest in Your Debt is unique and different from any other debt management/elimination or financial self-help book you may have read!

First, this book is different because it is not based simply on the "thinking" of some "self-appointed" expert who decides to write a book. Walk into any bookstore, check out Amazon.com or go to your local library and you will find many books from "financial gurus" who are surely well meaning people. But, how much of what they teach goes beyond theory and is based on their own "real world" experience?

The information in this book represents **tried and true methods and strategies**. *Invest in Your Debt* represents the best of the best. What we teach has been compiled from the best teachings from the best debt elimination teachers in the world today. It is the financial plan we ourselves follow.

We don't believe in debt management. Debt management means keeping debt and debt is the obstacle, the 800-pound gorilla that prevents most people from achieving true financial freedom. We believe in debt elimination. By investing in your debt first, and eliminating your debt, you can then begin traditional investing using the payment money you had been wasting on debt.

Several hundred people, including the authors of this book, teach *Invest In Your Debt* in colleges, universities, high schools, corporations, churches and any place where people who have this great debt opportunity gather. IYD, Inc., the publisher of this book, is the organization that provides the materials and the central point through which these teachers share their knowledge, ideas and experiences.

These teachers are on a mission. At one time, they were searching for financial solutions in their own lives and they attended a debt elimination class. For many of them, the class had such a profound impact on their financial lives that they have felt compelled to share this life-enhancing program with others. *Invest in Your Debt* has grown and evolved in their classrooms.

Therefore, this *Invest in Your Debt* book is the result of the experience of many teachers, teaching classes for tens of thousands of students. What we teach is real, not "pie-in-the-sky" theory. We especially welcome skeptics to bring their own debt numbers to class, so by the time they leave they have a written plan, based on their current financial situation that shows how IYD can work for them. We also know it works because we get letters, emails and phone calls from former students telling us about their success! In addition, of course, we know IYD works because of what it is doing for our teachers and ourselves. Check out the appendices in this book for some testimonials to the power of investing in your debt.

The second reason *Invest in Your Debt* is different from other financial self-help or debt-management/elimination books is that…

11

We actually teach a practical method for financial success which begins with eliminating your debt instead of simply preaching about the benefits.

The key word here is "practical." Many books teach how to invest wisely in pork bellies, real estate, the stock market and so forth. However, most families don't have enough money left over at the end of the month to really invest seriously. Investment advice doesn't do you much good if you don't have money to invest.

Most debt management/elimination books will tell you that you should spend less, carry less debt and have a six-month cash reserve, but they don't tell you how to do it! A few such books will provide a method for "how-to" eliminate your debt, but they offer no flexibility to handle changing circumstances. *Invest in Your Debt* also has a step-by-step process we refer to as the "linear math, variable path methodology." *Invest in Your Debt* is unique because the process we teach is flexible. It recognizes that "life happens" – financial surprises arise in the midst of any good plan. We teach you "how to" keep your debt elimination plan rolling along, even when surprises happen.

From our perspective, the most important aspect of any financial plan is not how long it takes, or whether one approach or another is promoted.

The most important aspect of a financial plan is "does it work?"

The fact of the matter is that most financial plans will work if people stick to the plan. The plan usually isn't the problem. Commitment to the plan is. Therefore, persistence is the real variable here.

With most plans, "Does it work?" really means "will people stick with it?"

Can people stick to the plan? Most financial plans are strict and rigid. We have learned over the years of teaching that in order to help as many people become financially free as possible, we need a plan that can adapt to changing circumstances. People cannot feel that the plan is "all or nothing" because then when something happens that wasn't planned for, it is too easy to give up on the plan. We don't want people to give up and say, "IYD doesn't work" when the first minor problem occurs. Without flexibility, giving up happens all too easily when things do not go exactly as planned.

For example, have you ever been on a strict diet? Perhaps it was one where you could not have any sweets. When you know you cannot have ice cream, doesn't that sometimes make you want it even more? So then if you decide, "Oh, one spoonful of ice cream won't hurt," doesn't that one taste often lead to more ice cream and then some more until finally you've finished all the ice cream? Now you think to yourself, "I knew that diet wouldn't work" as you begin looking for a bag of cookies.

Many diets today recognize that it is important that people not feel like they are denying themselves, so they allow "cheating." We don't want you to have something unexpected come up and then decide that "IYD doesn't work" because you can't follow the IYD plan and handle the "surprise" at the same time.

The debt elimination methodology at the heart of this program recognizes that intentional "cheating" does not destroy your plan, but it does require a balancing adjustment. For example, let's say your plan included an allowance for the purchase of a used car, but when the time came you instead bought a new car. That choice will not wreck your program, but it certainly will require an adjustment of how long it will take you to pay off all of your debts. Of course if you cheat all the time you'll never get out of debt. But we recognize that most everyone, ourselves included, will "cheat a little" every once in a while. Recognize the effects of that slip, make the adjustment, and move on. The important thing is to keep your eye on the prize – freedom from all debt and True Financial Freedom.

IYD is flexible because we realize that financial surprises come up in our lives, like needing new tires, a new refrigerator or some other household item. More importantly, with IYD, we encourage people to have fun!

You enjoyed getting into debt, didn't you? So you need to have fun getting rid of it as well!

You need to have fun while investing in your debt. If you don't enjoy getting out of debt, you won't stick to your plan. If you don't stick to the plan, you cannot eliminate your debt. If you don't eliminate your debt, compound interest will be working against you forever and you will not achieve true financial freedom.

Everything in IYD is based on simple mathematics. The mathematics can be summarized like this:

1) Compound Interest working against you (debt) will prevent financial freedom – when you pay compound interest you **make others wealthy.**

2) Compound Interest working for you (investments) will create true financial freedom – when you earn compound interest you **make yourself wealthy!**

Compound interest is much like fire. Fire isn't inherently good or bad, but it can cause good and bad outcomes. Think of the good fire does…it can warm your body…it can cook food…it can warm your house. But what else can fire do to your house? IT CAN BURN YOUR HOUSE DOWN TO THE GROUND!

Depending on how we handle fire, if we are careful or not, we can get different results from working with it. Compound interest is the same. When it works for us in investments, compound interest is terrific. When it works against us in debt, **Compound Interest can Burn Us! Big Time!**

The third reason *Invest in Your Debt* is different is because we take a positive approach. We don't want to make people feel bad about debt. We don't want people to feel like dummies and beat up on themselves. But we do want to wake people up to "The rest of the story." The way we do that is by focusing on debt as an investment opportunity, instead of a problem.

We want to set a tone, establishing a mindset for you when reading this book. Most people don't perceive debt to be a problem. Some don't even think of themselves as having a debt problem because they are able to make their payments. "Everyone else has debt, don't they? Heck, even our parents still make mortgage payments, lease cars and use credit cards." It is this type of "follow the crowd" thinking that contributes to the fact that most people would probably never read a book about debt elimination until…until a financial catastrophe strikes. Maybe an illness or a death in the family happens. Maybe someone loses a job or just starts worrying about saving for college for the kids or for retirement.

The bottom line is most people never look at debt as an obstacle to their financial success. Advertising has taught using credit cards is "smart money," getting a home equity loan is "cheap money." It is difficult to recognize the dangers of debt when we are bombarded with so many messages to the contrary.

E.G. Frank, one of our newsletter authors and teacher coined the term "intentional naivety." He uses this to describe the phenomenon of people who don't perceive their personal debt as a problem. As E.G. puts it, "most people are in a state of denial or avoidance about their finances. They are intentionally naïve. They avoid learning about finances because that lack of knowledge provides a handy excuse when they fail."

We know these people (who don't view debt as a problem) and most others can benefit from IYD because we have studied massive amounts of financial statistics. These statistics show a growing amount of debt and a shrinking amount of traditional savings and investing. People know they should invest, but they don't have any money left after making debt payments to work on building wealth. The statistics show that if people eliminate their debt, they will be able to achieve true financial freedom. We would rather have people learn of this debt opportunity before it becomes an emergency situation. This is why we hope to catch their interest, and maybe your interest, by explaining the process from an opportunity perspective.

This book is not written just for people who are having debt problems. In fact, quite the contrary is true. *Invest In Your Debt* is most beneficial for those people that are able to make their debt payments each month, but realize that they don't want to have to do that forever! They have spent years building up debt, and they now want it to go the other direction.

And what a great opportunity debt presents us when we look at it as an investment. What is an investment? It is something that you put money into and hope to get more money back in return. There are three benefits of the IYD process that make it a much more powerful investment than traditional investments. Traditional investments are considered very good if they average a 10% growth, or rate of return, over time.

In this book, you will learn that investing in your debt is such a powerful financial vehicle…

The typical family with IYD will get a 30% to 40% return on their investment!

Investing in your debt, for most people, allows your money to grow much faster than any other investment. Huge growth of your money is the first benefit of IYD. Now there are speculative investments that can generate larger returns, if you are lucky. If you are not lucky, you could lose all your money. But the second benefit of IYD removes the luck factor.

With IYD, the return is guaranteed!

This means that you don't have to worry about whether the stock market goes up or down. You don't have to wonder if you are going to make money or lose money. With IYD, as long as you follow your plan, the return is guaranteed. Now when you make money with a traditional investment, the taxman usually gets the government's share of your growth. But with the guaranteed growth of IYD, you get to keep all your money because…

Any return you earn with IYD is TAX FREE!

So with IYD, as compared to traditional investments, there are three primary benefits. You get a high rate of return so your wealth grows. Your return is guaranteed so you don't have to worry. Your return is tax-free so you get to keep all of the growth. We may be biased, but when you look at investments, it makes sense to say…

Investing in your debt is a great investment!

With the return, and the guaranteed growth and the lack of taxes, can you think of a better investment? For most people, investing in their debt is by far the best investment. There are two exceptions to this rule. First, if someone is currently able to save and invest all the money they need to achieve their financial goals, then they really don't need to do something different financially. Of course, IYD would still help them – they just don't need IYD to achieve their goals. The second exception is for people who have paid off all their debt. At that point they need to begin using traditional investments. We encourage people to invest in their debt as their first investment, but once you are debt free you can no longer invest in your debt!

By investing in your debt first, before rushing into pork bellies, mutual funds, stocks, etc., you can learn to enjoy life more. You will be able to SMILE MORE! You can have less stress and fewer financial problems. Does this sound like a dream? It doesn't have to be if you simply take advantage of the investment opportunity your debt presents you.

You have the opportunity to turn things around. You can go from one who pays compound interest to one who earns compound interest. Think of all the money you send out the door each month in the form of car payments, credit card payments, mortgage payments, loan payments, etc. How much better would your financial situation be if you could instead keep all that payment money for yourself? How would you be doing on your current income if you were debt free?

This is the IYD opportunity. Free yourself from the conventional wisdom that leads most people to financial failure. Follow the IYD process.

Eliminate your debt and then use the money you had been wasting on debt payments to create real wealth and achieve true financial freedom. The typical family can achieve debt freedom (and an important measure of financial freedom) in just five to eight years (even less if you don't have a mortgage). Best of all, you don't need to get a second job, live like a hermit in the Himalayas or a monk in the monastery. You can do this with the income you currently bring home!

Let that sink in for a minute. IYD offers the promise of true financial freedom based on your current income. How many times have you thought "I'll never get ahead until I make X dollars." Do you know of any other financial plan that can get you where you want to be financially based on your current income and expenses?

Please know that we are not solely focused on money. We don't believe that being financially free, wealthy, or well off is the objective of life. But most would agree, that if we have the money we need, if we decrease our money worries it is far easier to concentrate more on the important things in life like family, friends, charity work, etc.

The good news is this - for most of us, all the money we need already exists in our lives. We just need to re-channel it in a different direction. The process is here. You just simply need to decide how badly you want to change your current financial situation. If true financial freedom is important enough to you, you will find a way to make IYD work in your life!

We've been teaching people to invest in their debt for a number of years. Most people who come to our in-class workshops are searching for solutions to common financial problems and challenges. Here are some examples of the situations we see…

"I'm making a good income but can't seem to get ahead."

"I need to start saving for retirement or children's college or a down payment for a house, but there's never any money to do so."

"All of my money goes to bills – there's nothing left for me!"

Do any of these scenarios sound familiar? They all boil down to a common thread. People feel like they don't have enough money to achieve their goals. They feel like their finances are controlling their lives rather than them being in control of their finances. What's the solution? Should they get another job? Wouldn't things be better if they just could make more money? Maybe they just need to win the lottery and all their financial problems will disappear!

Our experience shows that "more money" is seldom the solution to financial problems. Don't take this the wrong way – making more money is great. But the real issue isn't how much money you make – the issue is how much is left at the end of the month after you pay your bills.

Most of us have been fortunate through our careers to see our incomes rise over time, even when inflation is factored in. Are you making more money now than you did five years or ten years ago? Most of us are making more money now, so wouldn't we expect to have more money left over at the end of the month?

The truth however is that for most people making more money hasn't helped them get ahead financially. As their income has risen so have their expenses! In fact, during the 1990s spending, or expenses, rose faster than incomes. This means as incomes rose, the amount of money left over at the end of the month actually decreased! What a diabolical correlation! Worse yet, many have had inflation eat up most if not all of their increases, necessitating second jobs, spouses having to work instead of staying home with the children and a lowering of expectations of what life may have to offer.

We see people in class who make $10,000 a year and people that make $250,000 and every income level in-between. Amazingly these folks all share one significant characteristic. The majority of their disposable income is being used to service their debt. This means that regardless of income, most people have about the same percentage of their income going towards debt.

This makes sense because one of the tools credit industry uses is the "debt-to-income" ratio in determining whether someone qualifies for credit. The creditors don't just care how much money you make – they also want to know what percentage of your income is going towards debt. Someone with a lower income can be a better credit risk than someone with a higher income if his or her ratio is better.

For example, let's say you have two people applying for a loan. Arnie Average makes $2000 per month and currently pays $500 on debt each month. Betty Bucks makes $5000 per month and pays $2000 on debt each month. Arnie has $1500 income left after debt payments while Betty has $3000, or twice as much income left after debt payments. Who do you think the creditors would be more likely to lend money to?

Though this is an oversimplification, Arnie is probably more likely to get additional credit because his debt to income ratio (debt payments divided by income or 500/2000) is 25%. Betty has a debt to income ratio of 40%. Most mortgage companies like to see these ratios under 40% (though we've seen people at 50% or more in class!)

This explanation about credit ratios is provided to make an important point…

The best way for most people, regardless of income, to improve their financial situation is to eliminate their debt!

We don't want people hung up on thinking "I don't make enough money to succeed financially." That's an excuse, a "cop-out," a justification for non-performance. If you really want to get ahead and make your financial future brighter for yourself and your family then read on. We let people know up front what they can expect.

You can be debt free in about five to eight years, including your student loans and mortgages. Once you are out of debt, you can continue to build real wealth by putting the money you were previously wasting on debt payments into traditional investments like the stock market or 401(k) accounts.

If you follow this *Invest in Your Debt* approach, at some point in time, you will no longer need to work to support yourself. Your investments will grow to a level where you can live off of the income they generate.

Does this sound too good to be true? Let's make it even better! You can do all of this with nothing more than your current income. You don't need a second job. You don't need to win the lottery. You don't need to live like a hermit in the Himalayas. True financial freedom is within your grasp, within your income and within your ability. All you have to do is reach out and grab it!

Near the beginning of an *Invest in Your Debt* class, we often sample the student's reaction and ask "How many of you are skeptical about these claims?" Usually a few brave souls raise their hands. You too might also have your hand up as you read this. We then joke with the class by saying "a few of you are a little skeptical so I guess that means the rest of you are extremely skeptical." More often than not, these people aren't just skeptical; they are gearing themselves up with every fiber of their being to **prove us wrong! (while being afraid to even hope that what we promise could actually be true for them).**

The promises we make about true financial freedom, freedom made possible by investing in your debt, intuitively go against everything we've been taught, read, heard or learned about money and finances. If what we teach in our classes is true, than everything (or most of what) we've learned is wrong!

We understand the skepticism. Most people consider themselves fairly knowledgeable about money and finances. They own a house, have a nice car or two, and pay their bills on time. Who are we to tell them they are doing everything wrong? Some people actually get angry and hostile when we present the "Rest of the Story."

Please understand that our purpose is not to condemn what anyone has done or to say they have made mistakes. But when you consider that even though personal income is higher than ever, people are having a harder time making ends meet, saving for retirement or college and bankruptcy rates are skyrocketing, may we suggest that there might be a better way than what conventional wisdom teaches. We believe that with consumer debt at an all time high, car leases growing at astronomical rates and less than 2% of the population actually **owning** their houses[1] (the rest of the houses are owned by the mortgage companies!), debt is having a devastating effect on typical families.

If what we say upsets you, it is not an uncommon reaction. The anger people feel when discovering the rest of the story about debt often comes when people realize how they have been misled by the credit industry. But please put your feelings aside while you read this book and try to absorb as much as possible. We are about to teach you what some call THE debt elimination system. We prefer to explain to people that what we really teach is how to invest in your debt, and turn your financial life around, regardless of your current situation. If you learn it and apply it to your life, it will be worth hundreds of thousands, even millions of dollars to you over your lifetime.

Now we know that at this point in the book not everyone is convinced they want to give up the convenience and bonuses of those credit cards or lose that sacred mortgage interest tax deduction. Before we get into the IYD process in class, we usually ask, "Do you want to achieve financial freedom?" Of course, everyone says "yes." In the book *The Millionaire Next Door*, we learn that financially successful people, that is millionaires, own their own homes and don't lease their cars. If you too say "yes" to financial freedom, then you must start acting like those who have already achieved it. You need to act like "the millionaire next door."

---

1 John Cummuta, *Debt-FREE & Prosperous Living*, 8th ed. (Boscobel, WI:Debt-FREE & Prosperous Living, Inc., 1998)

The key to financial freedom is to start by investing in your debt, so you can get your own risk-free, guaranteed, net of taxes 37.13% rate of return!

Let's start by getting the skepticism out of our systems…do any of these examples of skepticism sound familiar?

"There's no way I can get out of debt on my current income."

"It's impossible to pay off a 30-year mortgage in five to eight years."

"You can't achieve financial success without OPM (other people's money)."

These typical thoughts people have when first learning about IYD come straight from the "gospel" of conventional wisdom. We welcome the skepticism. Most of us who teach *Invest In Your Debt* once felt the same way. We also welcome the skepticism because we have a lot of fun with "conventional wisdom" in our classes.

People come into our classes, all charged up thinking "by golly who do they think they are, getting people's hopes up about getting out of debt – I'll show them – I'll prove they're wrong!!!!!" They are expecting a "catch." When people are unable to imagine how something can happen, they look for the "smoke and mirrors."

Well folks, let's be clear on this point. There really is no catch or smoke and mirrors. The *Invest in Your Debt* process is built on simple mathematics. And you will easily understand how the math works. It will make sense. You will realize that there is no magic, just a different way of looking at things. It really is common sense.

But common sense doesn't always impress people. We saw in our classes that teaching people to pay a little more on their debt and to focus on one debt at a time doesn't get people excited. Even though the process is just that simple, we decided to jazz things up.

So we applied a little bit of marketing common sense to the process. We now refer to the *Invest in Your Debt* process as a **LINEAR MATH, VARIABLE PATH METHODOLOGY**.

Chapter 2

Linear Math / Variable Path Methodology

Now that sounds powerful doesn't it? The phrase inspires people to believe that maybe there is a secret they didn't know about it. So over the years, the linear math, variable path methodology has become the core of the IYD process.

Let's get into the process, explain it, dissect and get it out of the way. I want you to see how it is absolutely mathematically possible for you to eliminate your debt as quickly as we promise. Of course, to make the possibility of debt elimination a reality, you need to go beyond the math, but the math is our starting point. You can eliminate your debt much faster than you ever imagined by simply investing in your debt. Best of all, you can do it all on your current income.

Here is an overview of the debt investing process. We start with the process in its simplest terms.

To invest in your debt…

STEP 1 –Pay off your smallest debt as fast as you can.

STEP 2 - Take the money you had been using to pay your smallest debt and ADD this money to the payment you are making on your second-smallest debt.

STEP 3 - When the second debt is paid off, take the payment money from the first and second debt, and add it to the payment you are making on your third-smallest debt.

STEP 4 - Continue this process until all your debts are paid, much faster than you could ever imagine.

This is simple common sense, folks. If you follow this debt investing process, you will eliminate all of your consumer debt (credit cards, car loans, student loans, etc.) in about one to three years. Then if you take the money you had been paying on consumer debt and add it to your 30-year mortgage payment, your mortgage will be paid off in just another four to five years.

This is the IYD process in its simplest form. It is your roadmap to true financial freedom. Of course, life isn't simple. There are many other considerations. Review the debt investing process and make sure you understand it. Then continue reading this chapter as we will add some real-world considerations to this process.

How does the Process Work?

"How can this really happen?" you ask. The key aspect that allows you to wipe out your debt FAST is FOCUS. Focus is a critical element of the debt elimination and debt investing process. What do we mean by focus?

Focus means keeping the money you are currently spending on debt **FOCUSED on debt until your debt is eliminated.** In other words, even when that first debt gets paid off, you should continue using the monthly payment from the first debt – just redirect that payment to another debt. This means the total amount you pay on your debt remains the same, even though you have one less debt now that the first is paid off.

Focus also means concentrating on one debt at a time: maximizing your payment on one debt. In order to "maximize your payment" on a debt you need to invest any "extra" money you have by adding it to the regular payment. Now we don't want you to have to worry about getting a second job in order to have "extra" money to invest in your debt. So where does this "extra" money come from? One of the places "extra" money comes from is payments you are making on other debt. When you pay off a debt, the money you had been using for payments on that debt is now "extra" money! What should you do with this newly found "extra" money? Invest it in your next debt!

This is what we mean by *Invest in Your Debt*. It's a guaranteed, risk-free investment. And we don't know of any bankers who won't take your money for the extra payment!

26

When you pay significantly more on a debt by increasing your payment with payment money from other paid-off debts you "short-circuit" the power of compound interest. Remember though, these increased payments aren't extra money coming out of your pocket – they are money shifted from other debt payments – money that you were already spending on debt. When you shift this money to other debts is when you truly begin to invest in your debt!

Unfortunately, for most people, when one debt gets paid off, they usually create a new debt and a new payment or that money gets spent in any number of ways. This is part of what we call the monthly payment trap. When we pay off a debt, the payment amount is often viewed as "now-available-to-spend" money. It's almost a family tradition that when we have room in our monthly budget we must find a bill to fill the budget! Think of it as the great debt treadmill. One debt falls off the back of the treadmill and a new one pops up on the front of the treadmill.

Obviously, we need to break the habit of our willingness to create new debt, once an old debt is paid off, if we want to become debt free. So the first rule of investing in your debt is:

Continue using the same total amount of money you had been spending on monthly debt payments, even as some of the debts are paid off.

By doing this, instead of simply spending money on payments, you are now investing in your debt.

Do you believe this process can work for you? Suspend your disbelief for a moment. In a few pages, we will show you how to calculate the amount of time it will take you to be out of debt. For the time being, let's focus on why this can work for you.

One of the great aspects of this process is that you simply take the money you are already spending on debt and use it a little differently. You don't need to increase your income to make this process work. You don't need to start eating macaroni and cheese for every meal. You actually don't even need to make more than your minimum monthly payments to get the program started.

IMPORTANT - If you are not able to make at least your minimum monthly payments then you are in a debt crisis situation. You can still eliminate your debt and begin investing in your debt. However, it will just take a little longer and will require assistance from a professional Financial Coach. Please finish reading the book so you understand our philosophy.

Assuming you are currently making at least minimum payments, to begin the IYD process all you need to do is make a commitment to take the same total monthly debt payment that you are currently making and invest it in your debt until your debts are gone. Could you do this for five years, eight years, or even 10 years if you had to?

Does that seem like a long time? You've probably been spending a fairly large amount of money on debt payments each month for some time now haven't you? In fact, your total monthly debt payment has probably not stayed the same, but in fact increased over the last few years, hasn't it? All we're suggesting you do is continue with the payments you are already making. You would do that even if you didn't follow the *Invest in Your Debt* plan!

Now this process makes a great deal of sense to most people. In fact, you may have heard of similar processes sometimes called "snowballing" your debt or "accelerating" your debt or "rolling up" your debt. The concept isn't new, so why doesn't everybody do this? Think for a minute about what most people do with payment money when they pay off a debt?

When most people pay off a debt, they usually create another debt and use the payment money for that!

When we pay off a debt, all of a sudden that money that had been going towards the payment is burning a hole in our pocket. It feels like we have extra money in our monthly budget. Many people are so excited when they pay off a debt, perhaps one they had been paying on for years, that they feel the need to celebrate! While there is certainly nothing wrong with celebrating a paid-off debt (in fact you will see that we encourage it), unfortunately many people celebrate by "splurging" and making a big purchase on credit! Obviously, if we create new debt as soon as we pay off an old debt, we will never get ahead financially. Therefore, you probably will not be surprised to learn that second rule of focus when eliminating or investing in your debt is…

To become debt free, you must first stop creating new debt!

This means that if you really want to get out of debt, if you really want to achieve true financial freedom, you need to live on a cash basis. This leads us to the third rule of focus…

You should only buy those things that you can afford to buy with cash!

WOW! That sure seems drastic doesn't it? Life without credit – "impossible" many say. It's not impossible however, if you use the IYD process. With IYD, you can stop using credit cards, **even when emergencies happen.** With IYD, the next time you buy a car you will know how to buy it with cash! You will learn how to break the home equity loan cycle that has crippled the financial future of so many families.

We have a whole chapter about how to live on a cash basis, even when emergencies happen. In that chapter, we also discuss how you stay on track with the *Invest in Your Debt* process so that you don't create new debt. So while we won't go into detail about it now, for the purpose of explaining the IYD process, it must be understood that in order to be successful, you need to stop creating new debt.

The fourth and final rule of focus which will help you get the most from investing in your debt is again a common-sense idea that you may be familiar with, but have not been successful in making it a part of your financial life. The fourth rule of focus is…

Take any extra money you have each month and use it to invest in your debt!

We call this extra money your Spend Smart Factor. Again, we will have more on this later, but suffice it to say that the more extra money you invest in your debt beyond your minimum payments, the faster you will get out of debt and the more interest you will save. This interest you save is part of the "return" you get on investing in your debt. This "saved" money can then be used for traditional investments or whatever you desire instead of giving that money away to the credit card and finance companies.

As you become more familiar with how the *Invest in Your Debt* program works, and become comfortable with it, you will notice a common theme…

The more you invest in your debt each month, the faster you will eliminate your debt and achieve true financial freedom!

Now you don't need to be a math whiz to understand why it takes increased debt payments to get out of debt sooner. But remember, we promised you wouldn't have to get a second job, live like a hermit in the Himalayas or eat macaroni and cheese like a college student. And you don't need to do any of this. To prove it, let's look at how this program works for the Spendsmart family, our typical family. They will…

Continue to use the money they are now wasting on debt, but simply re-direct it, in order to optimize their payments and get out of debt as soon as possible.

The Spendsmarts have the following debts and payments…

Debt	Balance	Monthly Payment	Interest Rate	Months to Pay Off
MasterCard	$972	$24	22.9	6 yr, 6 mo
Discover	$2,755	$41	9.9	8 yr, 2 mo
VISA	$4,286	$86	18.9	8 yr, 2 mo
Her Car	$8,150	$359	7.12	2 yr, 0 mo
His Car	$11,650	$308	12.60	4 yr, 0 mo
Home Equity	$31,242	$389	10.11	11 yr, 3 mo
Mortgage	$110,286	$757	7.11	28 yr, 1 mo
Totals	$169,341	$1964		

If they pay their debt off the "normal way" they will be paying for the next 28 years and one month.

If they follow the linear math, variable path process, and invest in their debt, spending the same $1964 they are now spending on debt each month…

They will be debt free in just 10 years and eight months!

Now if you have the choice of keeping your debt for the next 28 years, or keeping it for the next 11 years, which would you choose? (By the way, YOU DO HAVE A CHOICE!)

Let's walk through the details. If you are skeptical, you can use a financial calculator to follow our process through and you will see that our numbers are accurate!

If the Spendsmart family commits to the IYD plan, simply paying their debt as they have been, they will have her car paid off in two years. During this time, their total monthly debt payments remain at $1964 per month, the same as they always were. Once the car is paid off, they add the $359 they were paying on her car to their next smallest debt, the MasterCard. Watch how this process proceeds.

In this example, once our typical family's first debt, her car loan, is paid off they will use the approach of paying their debts off in priority order from the smallest balance debt to the largest balance debt. The first debt they invest in is referred to as priority one, the second as priority two, and so forth. So once the first debt is paid off, her car loan in this case (creating "extra" money), the smallest debt remaining, or the next priority debt is the MasterCard. If they take the extra $359 they had been spending on the car loan payment, and add it to their MasterCard payment of $24, their new MasterCard payments of $383 ($359 + $24) will have the MasterCard paid off in just another three months. Now two years and three months after they started investing in their debt, they have two debts paid off and are starting to make some real progress!

The next priority debt they will attack is the Discover card. The monthly amount they will invest in their Discover card is $424. This includes the extra $359 from her car payment, the extra $24 from the MasterCard payment and the $41 they had already been paying on the Discover card. Now the Discover card is paid off in just another five months. This is two years and eight months after they started their IYD program. By investing in their debt, the Discover card is paid off more than five years early!

(Actually, the credit cards are paid off more than 30 years early as you'll see in the chapter entitled "What Credit Card Companies Hope You Never Find Out!" but if we told you that now, you wouldn't believe us!)

Next, our typical family take the total "extra" payment of $424 that they had been paying on the Discover card and add it to their $86 Visa payment. By investing $510 into their Visa debt each month, the Visa card is paid off in just another seven months! Just like the Discover card, this is almost five years earlier than conventional wisdom!

Once her car and the credit cards are paid off, the Spendsmart family has an extra $510 each month to add to the $308 payment on his car. When they invest $818 each month into his car loan payment, the car is paid off only three months after the credit cards are paid off.

At this point, the Spendsmart family has been investing in their debt for three years and six months. But look what they have accomplished! They are miles ahead of the typical family in terms of their financial position. They have paid off all of their consumer debt, their two cars and three credit cards, way ahead of schedule. They have certainly saved money on interest, but more importantly they now have an "extra" $818 in their monthly budget. All of this was accomplished by just redirecting their debt payments and doing things a little differently than conventional wisdom would tell them.

Now, what about their mortgage? Typically, when people think about paying off their mortgage, the mortgage balance seems so large, and their ability to add extra payments so small, that the idea seems foolish and impossible. Once, however, someone has paid off all of their consumer (non-mortgage debt) like our typical family, they really have the ability (and extra payment money) to really make a dent in their first and second mortgages!

When they add this "extra" money to their home equity loan payment, they increase the monthly payment (or monthly investment) to a total of $1207. At this rate, it only takes them less than two more years to wipe out the home equity loan. The home equity loan is paid off six years and 11 months early.

Taking the final step to debt freedom, once the home equity loan is paid off, the Spendsmart family adds the $1207 to their mortgage payment. Remember, the $1207 is simply money that came from other debt payments they previously made. Again, our typical family doesn't have to find extra money in their budget to make this happen! They just redirect the $1207 from old debt payments and invest it in their mortgage.

When the Spendsmarts add the $1207 they had been spending on other debt payments to their regular mortgage payment of $757, investing $1964 into their mortgage loan each month eliminates their mortgage just five years and two months after they have paid off all their other debt. The mortgage is paid off in a total of 10 years and 8 months instead of 28 years and one month.

Now that the Spendsmart family is debt free, they have an "extra" $1964 in their monthly budget. Now they can use the money they had previously been wasting on debt to improve their financial situation even further. Just as important, they have saved $94,413 in interest! Ben Franklin says "a penny saved is a penny earned." $94,413 of earned (saved), or extra income is quite a return on their investment in their debt! Best of all, these earnings are tax-free! No one from the IRS can tax these earnings – do you think the same would be true of you earned an extra $94,413 from your job?

You can see that the aspect of "focus," where we continue to use all debt payment money as investments in debt until all debts are eliminated, can truly get people debt free quickly. Even better, this approach of "using the existing money differently" means you don't have to increase your income to get out of debt! You can invest in your debt, right now, with your current income! But hold on before you get too excited, because we're about to show you there are additional aspects of focus that can speed the debt elimination process even more!

Another aspect of "focus" is to maximize your payment on your first debt, again, not by earning more money, but by decreasing your payments on other debts. You see, for many people, "extra" money exists in your current payments.

Have you ever paid more than the minimum payment on any of your debts? Most people make "greater-than-minimum" payments on their debts. Most of us however, when we pay "extra" on debts, end up spreading the money over several debts. While on the surface this seems wise, and the intention is good, unfortunately this is the fastest, quickest way to nowhere!

In order to get out of debt as soon as possible, you need to stop paying extra on several of your debts and **MAKE MINIMUM PAYMENTS ONLY** on all but your first priority debt. We understand that it may seem contradictory to conventional wisdom to tell people to make minimum payments only. But the *Invest in Your Debt* process is much faster if you maximize payments on one debt, by minimizing payments on all other debt. In other words, if you are making extra payments on some debts, stop making those extra payments! Instead, invest all the extra payment money into your first priority debt. Once the priority one debt is paid, then begin to invest in the priority two (next smallest balance) debt.

Why do we want you to focus on one debt at a time, instead of investing extra in several at a time? In all reality, often the difference in interest saved and time to total debt-freedom will not be significant. What can be significant, however, is the excitement in getting that lowest balance debt paid off really quickly. That small step, in and of itself, helps set the tone for the remainder of your program! With a 10% Spend Smart Factor, the Spendsmart family gets their MasterCard paid off in just two months. Would they put just $100 of their Spend Smart Factor towards that card it would take nine months to pay off.

In our typical family example, however, they are not currently making extra payments. They are already pushed to their financial limit, so all of their payments are currently the minimum payment amount. They cannot speed the IYD process by taking extra money from other payments and investing it in their first priority debt.

There is another way that our typical family can increase the payment on their first debt and jump-start the *Invest in Your Debt* process. They can get out of debt even sooner than 10 years and eight months if they use the **SPEND SMART FACTOR!**

It's obvious that investing extra money into your debt can eliminate debt very quickly. One of our promises, however, is that you can follow the IYD plan without increasing your income. So if you don't increase your income, how can you increase the money you invest in your debt? The answer is Spend Smart!

One of the most frequent questions we get during our workshops is "How can I find the money to increase my debt payments, or to begin investing in my debt?" Because so many people were interested in this topic, and because the subject is so vast, we developed a class and text dedicated to the topic. While you will find a chapter on spending smarter in this book, let us give you a quick summary.

We all make financial choices every day. These choices usually involve spending. Such choices can range from small decisions like "should I eat breakfast before I leave for work or pick something up on the way" to large decisions such as "should I get a 15 or 30 year mortgage?" Spend Smart is a new approach to spending decisions.

Spend Smart focuses on how people can easily make small changes in their life in order to save money, without having to sacrifice their current lifestyle. In other words, you don't have to eat macaroni and cheese! Now knowledge about how to save money on spending is important, but don't most of us already have some good ideas on how to save money? We just need a good reason to dedicate ourselves to doing it. When you see how much impact a little money saved on spending can have on your IYD plan, trust us, you will be motivated!

More than just knowledge about how to save money on spending, Spend Smart is a process just like the IYD program is a process. The Spend Smart process turns the money you save on spending into cash in your hand at the end of the month. This cash in your hand is what you can use to put your IYD plan into high gear!

We know that most people have some "fat" in their spending. That is, they could make some different choices that would decrease their spending. If people choose to Spend Smart and their expenses are decreased, this makes more money available for investing in their debt. More importantly, these decreases in spending can be done without someone feeling like they are sacrificing or living like a pauper!

Spend Smart is not about doing without. It's about spending smarter to buy everything we need in life, not buying everything "they" want us to buy. If you buy everything they want you to buy, you'll have no money left at the end of the day, the end of the week, the end of the month – you'll have nothing left at the end of your life!

Therefore, we call the extra money people invest in their debt the Spend Smart Factor. If people want to get out of debt as quick as possible, how big should their Spend Smart Factor be? The larger the Spend Smart factor, the sooner you will be out of debt and therefore, financially free. Financial planners talk about "paying yourself first" with 10% of your monthly gross income when working towards financial freedom. For the purpose of showing how much of a difference the Spend Smart Factor can make when investing in your debt, we will use the same 10% figure that the financial planners use. For your personal IYD plan, you can use 10% of monthly gross income, 10% of monthly net income, 20% or 2% or whatever you want. Remember, the IYD process is about choices and it is your choice!

Let's look at how a 10% Spend Smart Factor affects the typical family's IYD plan. Remember their current debt items:

Debt	Balance	Monthly Payment	Interest Rate	Months to Pay Off
MasterCard	$972	$24	22.9	6 yr, 6 mo
Discover	$2,755	$41	9.9	8 yr, 2 mo
VISA	$4,286	$86	18.9	8 yr, 2 mo
Her Car	$8,150	$359	7.12	2 yr, 0 mo
His Car	$11,650	$308	12.60	4 yr, 0 mo
Home Equity	$31,242	$389	10.11	11 yr, 3 mo
Mortgage	$110,286	$757	7.11	28 yr, 1 mo
Totals	$169,341	$1964		

Their first priority debt is the MasterCard because it has the smallest balance. If they use Spend Smart and decrease their expenses without living like hermits, they can find an extra 10% in their income. This creates a monthly cushion of $427. This is the same $427 dollars the financial planners want you to invest with them. We say pay yourself first, by first investing in your debt. Once you have eliminated your debt, then you may need a financial planner to help with your traditional investments. But we can teach you how to make your first investment with the IYD program. So when the Spendsmart family uses the Spend Smart Factor, they can begin the IYD process by immediately investing extra money in their debt.

When our typical family increases their MasterCard payment from $24 to $451 by finding a 10% Spend Smart Factor, the MasterCard gets paid off in three months instead of 6 ½ years. Next they move the focus of investing in their debt to the Discover card.

Adding their new "extra" money of $451 to their $41 Discover payment, the debt is paid off five months later. Eight months into the process at this point, the Spendsmarts now have $492 "extra dollars" to continue to invest in their debt.

The next priority debt (smallest debt remaining) is the Visa card. Using their new debt cushion of $492 and adding it to their $86 Visa payment, the Visa is eliminated eight months later. So, by just creating a 10% Spend Smart Factor, our typical family has eliminated their $8013 credit card debt in just one year and four months!

After the credit cards are paid off, the Spendsmarts now have an extra $578 to invest in her car loan. After making payments of $937 on her car each month, the car is paid off in only three more months.

Rolling the debt cushion up to his $308 car payment increases the investment in Mr. Spendsmart's car loan to $1245. At this level, his car is paid off in six more months. At this point, the typical family is two years and one month into the process. After only two years and one month of following the IYD process, the Spendsmart family has surpassed most families in terms of their financial situation by completely eliminating their consumer debt.

After two years and one month, their debt consists of only their mortgage and home equity loan. Better yet, they have $1245 available each month to invest in their mortgages. Compare this to the first example where the typical family had all their consumer debt paid off in three years and six months by following the IYD plan, but without using the Spend Smart Factor. Now this is much better than paying off debt the way conventional wisdom teaches, but notice how the Spend Smart factor greatly accelerates the process.

Next, the Spendsmart family will invest their debt cushion of $1245 into the home equity loan. Raising their home equity payment from $389 to $1634 wipes out the home equity loan in another 18 months. Then, adding the $1634 to the $757 mortgage payment will destroy the mortgage in just another four years and three months.

Using the 10% Spend Smart Factor allows the Spendsmart family to eliminate all their debt in only seven years and 11 months. This is 20 years and two months faster than if they had paid off their debt the conventional way. By investing their 10% Spend Smart Factor in their debt, they have saved (and therefore earned) $118,525 in interest. What a great investment!

Without a Spend Smart Factor, our typical family can get out of debt in 10 years and eight months and save (earn) $94,413 in interest. With a 10% Spend Smart Factor, they find a way to save $427 each month on their spending, they invest this money in their debt, and they get out of debt two years and nine months sooner and save an additional $24,112 in interest. Is it worth it to learn Spend Smart in order to get out of debt that much faster? Let's look at the facts.

	IYD Only	IYD + Spend Smart
Income	$51,188	$51,188
Monthly Debt Payment	$1,964	$1,964
Spend Smart Factor	$0	$427
Time to Debt Freedom	10 years, 8 months	7 years, 11 months
Total Payments	$251,392	$227,145
Total Interest Saved	$94,413	$118,525

So, what is the value of the Spend Smart Factor? Well first, you get out of debt (which is level one of true financial freedom) about three years sooner. Second, you save an additional $24,112 in interest payments (which is really the same as earning an extra $24,112, isn't it? Actually, it's even better…saving $24,112 in interest payments is the same as earning an additional $33,998 when you understand the replacement value of a dollar as we explain in Spend Smart). That's not all bad is it? And it can be done simply by using the 10% of your income that financial planners tell you to pay yourself with first.

We suggest you follow traditional financial planning advice literally – pay yourself first by investing in your debt.

Do you get the idea that we want you to find a Spend Smart Factor of 5%, 10%, 20% or more? We are guilty as charged. Besides the fact that it speeds your debt investment program, there is another central reason why we encourage people to find a Spend Smart Factor.

Spend Smart teaches you how to have a little less money leaving your household each month than you have coming in. In simple terms, it is about how to spend just a little bit less than you make. Does this sound over-simplified? Of course everyone knows that you need to spend less than you make. But what good does saving a little money on spending really do?

If we want to be financially successful, it makes sense to look at what others who are already financially successful have done. Would you agree that millionaires are financially successful people we might want to learn from? According to author Thomas Stanley, Ph.D., the number one most common trait amongst millionaires is that they spend a little less than they make.[2]

We know from experience that once you are able to consistently spend a little less than you make, you can change your financial future. If you are going to eliminate your debt, we want you to be able to stay debt free once you get there. Spend Smart not only helps you invest in your debt; it helps you stay debt free.

You see, money problems are typically not caused by a shortage of income. Rather, they are caused by too many expenses.

2Thomas J. Stanley and William D. Danko, *The Millionaire Next Door* (New York, NY: Pocket Books, 1998)

Are you familiar with the "rest of the story" regarding lottery winners? Many lottery winners end up broke only a few short years after winning. These people all of a sudden had more money than they had ever imagined. Unfortunately, this extra money didn't solve their financial problems; it just increased their spending. Since they had never learned how to keep expenses just a little below income, the amount of income they had did not matter. They continued to spend a little more than they had.

So the first reason we want you to learn Spend Smart is to make sure once you achieve debt freedom, you continue on the road to true financial freedom. Now we realize that's not really a reason you can sink your teeth into. There is another reason why you should learn Spend Smart – and it is measurable in terms of dollars and cents.

We encourage people to begin building wealth by first investing in their debt, and once they are out of debt by putting money into traditional investments. The problem is most people never have any money left at the end of the month for investing. But once the Spendsmart family has eliminated their debt, they now have the opportunity to invest the money they had previously been wasting on debt payments. This is where IYD really pays off with financial leverage!

Let's look at what the Spendsmarts can do in terms of real wealth building once they have finished investing in their debt. To add perspective, we will look at what our typical family can do financially, using their current income and IYD, as compared to what conventional wisdom tells them to do.

	Conventional Wisdom	IYD Only	IYD + 10% Spend Smart Factor
Time to Debt Freedom	28 years 1 month	10 years 8 months	7 years 11 months
Years/Months Saved	N/A	17 years 5 months	20 years 2 months

One of the keys to building real wealth is time. The longer an investment is allowed to grow, the more it will grow. This makes the "time saving" aspect of IYD so powerful. The more time you save by investing in your debt, the more time you have for maximizing traditional investments. This is where you have compound interest and the time value of money really beginning to work for you instead of against you (as it does when you have debt).

The Spendsmart family can follow conventional wisdom and have their debt paid off in 28 years and one month, assuming they create no new debt (and how likely is that?). By investing in their debt however, they can be out of debt 17 years and five months sooner. Over these 17 years they save, they can use the money they would have been wasting on debt if they had followed conventional wisdom, and invest it in traditional ways. How much is it worth to invest in your debt? Look at this table…

	Conventional Wisdom	IYD Only	IYD + 10 % Spend Smart Factor
Years/Months Saved	NA	17 years 5 months	20 years 2 months
Monthly Debt Payment	$1964	$1964	$1964
Investment Value*	$0	$1,099,638	$1,520,305

*NOTE – the investment value is calculated by investing the monthly debt payment into traditional investments ($1964) for the number of years and months saved. We assume a 10% growth rate on traditional investments.

If our typical family follows the basic process, they will be out of debt in just 10 years and eight months.

By first investing in their debt, they now have the choice to use their debt payments for traditional investments.

Once they are out of debt, if they then invest their debt payments over the same period of time when conventional wisdom would simply have them paying their mortgage "the conventional way," they will BECOME MILLIONAIRES!

The Spendsmart family has choices…

1) They can continue making their $1964 debt payments the normal way for 28 years and one month as conventional wisdom teaches and get out of debt, maybe…

OR

2) They can first invest in their debt, eliminate their debt in 10 years and eight months, then invest the $1964 they had been paying on their debt for the next 17 years and five months and build $1,099,638 in real wealth…

OR

3) They can first invest in their debt, use a 10% Spend Smart Factor, eliminate their debt in seven years and 11 months, then invest the $1964 they had been paying on their debt for the next 20 years and two months and build $1,520,305 in wealth…

There are some important points to remember here. First, the same family has the same income and expenses in all three scenarios, they are just using their money differently. Second, we are looking at their financial situation over the number of years they would have normally paid off their mortgage. What all this shows us is powerful in its simplicity…

With IYD, the typical family can become millionaires in the same amount of time they would have normally been struggling to pay off their mortgage, using just the money they are currently spending on debt!

WHAT A CHOICE! Should I follow conventional wisdom and own my home in 28 years and one month? Or should I Invest in my Debt and own my home in less than eight years PLUS HAVE A MILLION DOLLARS IN WEALTH in 28 years?

Let's go back to the question of whether learning Spend Smart is worth your time. Notice on the chart above, when our typical family uses a Spend Smart Factor, they accumulate even more wealth! In fact, they end up with $420,667 more. Why is this? It's the time value of money.

Even though in both examples, our typical family is investing the same $1964 each month, when they use IYD with a 10% Spend Smart Factor, they get out of debt two years and nine months sooner than when they use IYD alone. Now while two years and nine months doesn't seem like that much time, when you factor in the power of compound interest, that extra time translates into over $400,000 in additional wealth! Does that make using a Spend Smart Factor worthwhile?

Actually, the benefit of a Spend Smart Factor is even larger. Consider the fact that if our typical family creates a 10% Spend Smart Factor, by reducing expenses without decreasing their lifestyle, they have an extra $427 to invest in their debt each month as compared to what they would have to invest in their debt without a Spend Smart Factor. This means they are investing a total of $2391 in their debt each month.

Although this $2391 is $427 more than they pay on debt without a Spend Smart Factor, they have become accustomed to investing this amount in their debt each month. Once the Spendsmarts are out of debt in seven years and 11 months, all of this $2391 they were investing in their debt becomes available to invest in traditional investments. For comparison purposes, doesn't it make sense to assume that since they were investing $2391 into their debt each month that they will continue to invest the same amount when they begin using traditional investments?

Let's look at the wealth-building comparison from above again. But this time we will assume that if our typical family decides to create a 10% Spend Smart Factor, they will continue to use the 10% Spend Smart Factor as part of their traditional investment money, once they are out of debt.

	Conventional Wisdom	IYD	IYD + Spend Smart
Years/Months Saved	NA	17 years 5 months	20 years 2 months
Monthly Debt Payment	$1964	$1964	$2391
Investment Value	$0	$1,099,638	$1,850,840

How about that? When you include the 10% Spend Smart Factor, the Spendsmarts are able to create $1,850,840 in wealth, in the same amount of time they would have normally been struggling to pay off their mortgage. This is $751,202…three-quarters of a million dollars, more than they would build in wealth without a 10% Spend Smart Factor. So what is the value of the Spend Smart Factor for our typical family? Is it not proper to say…

The Spend Smart Factor is worth $751,202 to the typical family who decides to invest in their debt.

What about the typical family, who is following conventional wisdom as shown in the first column of the table above? They don't know the "Rest of the Story" as you are learning. If you are starting to see the power of this program, maybe you will teach those you love and care for about how to invest in their debt. They would certainly be grateful because…

The *Invest in Your Debt* program combined with the Spend Smart Factor is worth $1,850,840 to the typical family who is following conventional wisdom about debt!

If someone is paying their debt the "normal" way, what happens if they decide to use IYD and the 10% Spend Smart Factor? Using nothing more than their current income, the typical family can get debt free in about eight years and then create 1.85 million dollars in wealth in the same time they would have just been struggling to pay off their mortgage.

Do you have any doubt that IYD is extremely valuable to people? Do you see how the typical family can truly get ahead financially, regardless of their income? They simply turn the power of compound interest into a power that is working for them instead of against them.

Another way to look at IYD is to describe it as a process through which you create wealth from the depths of debt. Look at the numbers. At the beginning of the process, the Spend Smart family has $169,341 in debt. Seven years later they have no debt. Twenty years after that, they have $1,850,840 in wealth! Now that's a trade-off we hope everyone reading this book can get excited about!

SUMMARY

Let's do a quick review of the *Invest in Your Debt* program.

First, you want to FOCUS your efforts on paying off your debts in a specific order. You number your debts 1, 2, 3, 4, etc. This is the variable path methodology, deciding what debts to invest in, in what order. The variable path methodology can also be called prioritization. You want to make minimum payments on all debts other than your top priority debt. You choose the debt to pay off first (for simplicity, we suggest paying off the debt with the smallest balance first though we will discuss other methods of prioritization in the chapter on advanced IYD strategies).

You begin making payments (investments) as large as possible on your first priority debt. This means adding "extra" money to your payment. Where does this extra money come from? It can come from a variety of sources. It could be money that you were paying beyond the minimum payments on other debts. It could be money that comes from your Spend Smart Factor. It could be money that you were saving for a rainy day, money that comes from changing your W-2 withholding; it could be money from a tax refund. Remember however, even if you can find NO EXTRA PAYMENT MONEY you can still get out of debt much faster than conventional wisdom teaches by following IYD!

Once the first priority debt is paid off, you rollover your payment money from debt one, and add it to the minimum payment you have been making on priority debt two. When debt two is paid off, you rollover the payment money from debt two and add it to the minimum payment you have been making on priority debt three. This is the linear math portion of the IYD process, where compound interest begins working in your favor. You continue this process of taking the money you are investing in debt and rolling it over to the next priority debt once the previous debt is paid off.

In order to eliminate your debt as soon as possible, it is important that no new debt be created. This means you need to operate on a cash basis. Our program will help you learn how to live on a cash basis. Now the idea of living on cash basis, creating no debt, can seem impossible to people. It is of course easier to live on a cash basis if you build a small cash reserve for emergencies. If you have a cash cushion, then you don't need credit as much as you once thought you did, do you? We will talk about living on a cash basis and building a cash cushion in a later chapter.

So that's the overview of the linear math, variable path methodology. Make sure you understand the basics first. Once you understand the basics, move on to the chapter entitled "Advanced IYD Strategies." There we will examine the process more thoroughly, so you can figure out how to best apply the IYD program into your lifestyle.

Chapter 3

The Spend Smart Factor

There is no better place to invest than to invest in your debt. Once people see the IYD program they are amazed at how simple it is and how much sense it makes as a plan for financial freedom. Investing in your debt and getting a 37.13% return, risk-free, guaranteed and net of taxes is the best investment in the world! It is the best-kept secret on the planet.

For many people, learning about the IYD program is an epiphany – they suddenly "see the light!" Even once people agree that the program makes sense however, there is still some resistance. Many people feel uncertain about whether they can really do it.

If you feel this way, don't worry. IYD sounds good on paper and it is good in real life. In fact, doesn't it almost seem like it is "too good to be true?" When something sounds too good to be true, we tend to be skeptical, don't we? It is a normal human reaction.

We are on a mission to free this planet from debt. We want to help you achieve true financial freedom. Understand however, our plan is only a small part of the picture. The most important component of the program is your attitude.

You see, you are on the verge of beginning a journey to true financial freedom. Think about that for a moment. If you really believe financial freedom is within your grasp, if you really believe you have the chance to own your life again, are you going to let anything stand in your way?

Most people, at least initially, don't completely believe they can achieve financial freedom. So until you reach the point where you have absolute confidence in this program, we want to help you avoid excuses for failure.

We want to help guard against "excuses for doing nothing." One of the biggest excuses people give for not taking charge of their financial futures, for not implementing this program and starting to invest in their debt is

Yeah sure…IYD sounds good…but it won't work for me, because I never have <u>any extra</u> money! I can't find a Spend Smart Factor!

We understand this reaction. In our experience having had tens of thousands of people attend our workshops, it is important to let you know…

Everyone can find a 10% SPEND SMART FACTOR!

The real question is "Will you?" not "Can you?" Life is about choices as is this program. Do you choose to find 10 cents out of every dollar you earn to change the financial direction in your life or do you choose to continue your current financial path?

Now before we show you how easy it is to find Spend Smart Money, let's highlight one other important point about Investing in Your Debt. Some of you, after reading this chapter, will still be convinced that you do not have a Spend Smart Factor. We don't want anyone to let that lame excuse prevent them from changing their lives.

We've taught you the debt elimination / investment plan, using a 10% Spend Smart Factor. What if we teach you everything we know about finding Spend Smart Money and you still don't have a dime of your Spend Smart Factor? Guess what folks – it's okay because…

<u>**Investing in your debt works even if your Spend Smart Factor is $0!**</u>

How can that be? Are we saying that even if you cannot add any extra money to your debt payments you can still invest in your debt? Absolutely! If all you can do is make your minimum payments then you can still succeed with this opportunity!

Remember, the first example we show for the typical family in the Linear Math / Variable Path chapter is one where they add no extra money to their monthly debt payments. They were still able to invest in their debt, get compound interest working for them, and achieve debt freedom in about 11 years, using nothing more than the money they were currently wasting on debt. It just takes more time to accomplish this and you don't build as much wealth, but it still beats conventional wisdom.

It's human nature to take the path of least resistance. To do whatever is easiest. We inherently resist change. Implementing this program requires a few choices and changes. The easiest choice to make is to not change. We don't want you to fall into this tempting trap. Therefore we want you to understand…

You get to decide how quickly you will get out of debt and how much wealth you will build based on the size of your Spend Smart Factor you choose to find.

It really is all about choices. You already know that as long as you choose to invest in your debt, even if your Spend Smart Factor is $0, you are way ahead of the game. But every dollar you can add to your Spend Smart Factor has a significant impact on the IYD process. Let's look at how various Spend Smart Factors affect your financial freedom plan.

Spend Smart Factor	Spend Smart Money	Time until Debt Free
0%	0$	10 years, 8 months
5%	$214	9 years, 1 month
10%	$427	7 years, 11 months
20%	$854	6 years, 5 months

Though we believe everyone can find at least a 10% Spend Smart Factor, maybe you have chosen to start with a 5% Spend Smart Factor. That gets you out of debt 1½ years sooner than if you don't invest a single additional penny into your debt. For most people, once they are out of debt, they have much more freedom in their lives.

For example, once most people are debt free, they don't have to worry about losing their jobs. Not that they would want to, but if they did it isn't a financial catastrophe. They can work at a fast food restaurant and earn enough to pay the electric bill, put gas in the car and feed their families if they need to. Have you ever worried about what might happen if the company you work for is bought or merges with another company? Have you ever been downsized? Even in today's modern workplace, thousands of good, loyal employees lose their jobs everyday through no fault of their own.

With a 5% Spend Smart Factor, you will be free from the fear of losing your job 19 months sooner. Is that freedom from fear worth finding an extra $214 (5%) in your spending each month to invest in your debt? We can't answer the question for you, but that's the choice you have. Maybe the freedom from fear of losing your job gets you so motivated that you'll find a 20% Spend Smart Factor and get debt free more than four years faster than you would with a 0% Spend Smart Factor.

Obviously the amount of Spend Smart Factor impacts how quickly your debt is eliminated. But there is another reason why you may want to find as large of a Spend Smart Factor as possible. That reason is wealth creation. One of the greatest benefits of the *Invest in Your Debt* program is the opportunity it gives you to invest money, LARGE AMOUNTS OF MONEY, into traditional investments. Once you are debt free, you can then use all the money you had been spending on debt payments for investment in stocks, mutual funds, bonds or any investment of your choice.

What is truly amazing about Investing In Your Debt is…

You can actually begin creating great wealth in just the time you would have normally paid off your mortgage!

To look at the wealth-building potential of IYD, lets calculate how much true wealth our typical family can build by using the money they were first investing in their debt. We will have them use traditional investments during the time they pay off their debt and the time conventional wisdom would have them just paying on their mortgage.

If they didn't invest in their debt, it would take them 28 years and one month to pay off their mortgage. The sooner they complete the IYD program, the sooner they can begin building wealth with traditional investments. Because of the time value of money, the sooner you start building real wealth, the more wealth you will build. So how do different Spend Smart Factors affect the amount of wealth you can build? Look at the chart below:

Spend Smart Factor	Time Needed to Eliminate Debt	Time Available for traditional investing	Wealth Created
0% - $0	10 years, 8 months	17 years, 5 months	$1,099,638
5% - $214	9 years, 1 month	19 years, 7 months	$1,472,362
10% - $427	7 years, 11 months	20 years, 9 months	$1,850,840
20% - $854	6 years, 5 months	22 years, 3 months	$2,587,303

With a 0% Spend Smart Factor, you have the opportunity to build $1,099,638 in real wealth during the time you would have normally just been paying on your mortgage. Of course, if you can create a 10% Spend Smart Factor, you can build $1,850,840 in real wealth in the same amount of time. That's $750,000 more in wealth! Whether you get that extra three-quarters of a million dollars simply depends on your choices. Ask yourself this:

Is an extra $751,202 in wealth enough to motivate you to do what it takes to find a $427 Spend Smart Factor each month?

The math is simple, and it emphasizes the power of compound interest working for you. Many of us can easily let a few hundred bucks slip through our fingers each month. If instead you find a way to Spend Smart and hang on to an extra $427, you'll be a millionaire in 23 years. Does 23 years sound like a long time? Perhaps, but consider what other options you have for becoming a millionaire in the next 23 years!

Now that you have a better idea of how much a Spend Smart Factor can mean to your financial future, let's look at the big question…

How Can I Create a Spend Smart Factor?

There are many ways to create your Spend Smart Factor. There are general approaches you can take whose impact on your Spend Smart Factor will vary depending on circumstances. There are very specific actions you can take which we discuss in great detail in the book *Spend Smart, Creating Wealth Even With No Room in Your Budget.*

Before you start looking for ways to create your Spend Smart Factor, you have to get your attitude in the right place. For most people, when you talk about ways to save money on spending, their eyes glaze over and they take the attitude that it doesn't matter, "because it's just a few bucks." You need to really understand how the Spend Smart Factor makes a significant difference in your ability to achieve true financial freedom.

You see, it's all about leverage. There are many ways to save money on spending. You can cancel your movie channels on cable. You can brown bag lunch to work once or twice a week. You can raise your insurance deductible. You can cancel extended warranties. But these ideas themselves don't necessarily save enough money to really get people excited. It is when you leverage the savings with the *Invest in Your Debt* process that things get really exciting!

Consider a few of what we call the "Spend Smart Laws of Finances."[3]

"Most purchasing decisions are driven by emotion!"

When you think about ways to save money on spending, it often makes us feel like we will be depriving ourselves. We don't want to do without. You have to get past this emotion to successfully create a Spend Smart Factor. Instead of focusing on the negative emotion of "doing without" when working on your Spend Smart Factor you should focus on the positive of all

---

3 Bill Keenan, *Spend Smart, Creating Wealth Even With No Room In Your Budget* (Invest In Your Debt, Inc, 1999)

the wealth you can create simply by using a Spend Smart Factor to invest in your debt.

So let's say you do start finding ways to save money without drastically affecting your lifestyle. Have you ever saved money on spending before? For example, did you ever save $10 at the grocery store by using coupons? Many people have. The important question is, after making all that effort to save $10 on groceries, at the end of the month, when you check your wallet, do you still have that $10 you saved? If saving money on spending doesn't give you cash in your hand to invest in your debt at the end of the month, then there really is little benefit to spending smart.

Here's another Spend Smart Law of Finances…

"The only way to turn Spend Smart into cash is to seize your savings!"

What we mean by this is simple. Once you do something to save money, you need to take the money you saved and "hide it." You need to put it someplace where you won't be tempted to spend it. Apply the "out of sight, out of mind" principle to your Spend Smart Factor.

This may seem like a silly mind game. But guess what – it is another thing that our millionaire friends do. They apply a concept known as "false economic scarcity."[4] How do millionaires spend a little less than they have? They simply pretend that they have less money than they do!

We know it can be a bit of a transition to go from spending everything we make (and more) to spending less than we make. It is this type of spending behavior that has contributed to the record high debt levels. When you spend more than you make, it usually means you have to increase your debt to do so.

People may worry that they won't be able to survive while spending less than they have been. If you feel that way, think about a 401(k) account for a

---

4 Thomas J. Stanley and William D. Danko, *The Millionaire Next Door* (New York, NY: Pocket Books, 1998)

minute. Most people who put money into a 401(k) have this money deducted from their paycheck. At first they are worried that they won't be able to get along without the extra $50 or $100 in each check. But an amazing thing happens due to what is known as the elasticity of spending. This is expressed in one additional Spend Smart Law of Finances…

"Spending increases or decreases as available income increases or decreases!"

You know this intuitively, don't you? In general, what happens when you have some extra money, such as a tax refund? Most people spend it! What happens to spending on optional items, like eating out, if you have some surprises expenses in a month? Spending decreases!

The bottom line, folks, is that financial freedom is a choice. Perhaps in the past you have tried to improve your financial situation by "spending smart." You probably became frustrated because the relatively small amount of money you could save on your spending didn't make a big difference in your life. This is where *Invest in Your Debt* can make a difference. If you can find just a little bit of money and begin building a Spend Smart Factor, you can leverage this relatively small amount of money into true financial freedom!

So where can we start finding Spend Smart Factor money? Here are seven easy methods for finding Spend Smart Factor money. Let's take a look!

Spend Smart Factor Finder Method # 1 – Stop Making More Than Minimum Payments

As discussed in the chapter about our linear math / variable path process, the fastest way to get out of debt is to invest every extra dime you have into one debt at a time.

Any money you are currently paying above minimum payments on any debt is Spend Smart Factor money!

So if you are currently making more than minimum payments, all of that more-than-minimum-payment money goes towards your Spend Smart Factor! Now that method is pretty easy and most people feel comfortable using this method. This next one can be a little controversial though…

Spend Smart Factor Finder Method # 2 – Stop Saving!

Let's clarify our terms here. What we don't mean is "stop saving on spending." What we mean is stop putting money into savings plans, especially those that have no tax benefits like 401(k) or IRA plans have.

Are you putting money into a mutual fund, a Christmas club, buying savings bonds or putting money into a bank account? If you are putting money into some type of savings plan, we certainly congratulate the effort. Unfortunately, such types of "investments" are usually very unproductive for most people.

For most people, the best financial strategy is to first invest in your debt!

If we assume that people want to get the most from their money, investing in your debt is the way to get the best return. Read Appendix A7 and Appendix A13 to understand where we get the numbers for the return you get when you invest in your debt.

When you invest in your debt, you get a 37.13% rate of return. This return is guaranteed and net of taxes.

Now think about it – can you get this type of return on any other investment? If you have a regular savings account at the bank, you might get 1% to 3% return, or growth on your savings. If you have a money market account you might get 3% to 7% return. If you have money in a great mutual fund, you will get over a 10% return in the long term. Investing in your debt beats the return on all of these.

So if you are saving money in low return vehicles – STOP SAVING – use the money you are putting into savings and invest in your debt instead.

Because there is such a great return when you invest in your debt, it would be great if we could get that return forever. Eventually your debt will be eliminated however. That is the time when you need to maximize your investments in the traditional vehicles.

IMPORTANT NOTE – If you are currently putting money into a 401(k) or an IRA account, we suggest you continue to do so, especially to the extent your contribution is being matched by your employer. We believe a 10% Spend Smart Factor can be found without touching your 401(k) / IRA contributions. Even though you would probably get a better return by investing in your debt, you have started a good habit, and we don't want you to break it. We just want to help you start some additional good habits. As this book is about choices, it must be your final decision, because it is your debt.

Spend Smart Factor Finder Method # 3 – Cash in your safety net

Some people have "rainy day" funds, money stuck aside for future purposes, perhaps for emergencies, other than retirement plans. This type of money is often called a "safety net." Most of us have been taught we need a "safety net" equal to six months of living expenses. This money is usually in accounts like we talked about on the previous page, CDs, money market accounts, mutual funds, etc. Or it may be stuffed under a mattress!

People in our classes often ask "I have $5000 in a bank account – should I invest that money in my debt?" Our answer is ABSOLUTELY YES! If you have money in any type of liquid account, accounts other than a 401(k) or an IRA or any other tax-qualified plan, you should consider investing that money in your debt. Giving your IYD program a jump-start by investing a lump sum of money in your debt at the beginning of the process can make a huge difference.

How much of a difference can it make? Let's look at what would happen with the Spendsmart family if they had a $5000 safety net and they chose to invest it in their debt. They would be debt free in just seven years and seven months, four months faster than without the $5000 jump-start. More importantly, they can build $1,922,994 in true wealth, $72,154 more than they would without the $5000 jump-start.

Some people are comfortable with the idea of cashing in their safety net because they know once they are debt-free, they will not need a safety net anymore. Others however are not comfortable with the idea. In the chapter about Living on a Cash Basis, we do suggest a small cushion for handling emergencies. This idea of a six-month cash cushion however, is in most cases a concept that slows your journey to true financial freedom.

When were you first told you should have a six-month safety net? Was it last year? Five years ago? Ten years? Twenty? Since we've known about needing a safety net for the last twenty years or more, then surely most of us already have one, don't we? It probably won't surprise you to learn that when we ask in our workshops how many people have the six-month safety net, very few do. In fact, based on our classes, we estimate that the number of people who have the six month cushion is 2%, or about the same number of people who actually own their homes. (Hmmm…is there a connection there?)

So if we've known for many years that we should have a six-month safety net, but we still don't have one, does it make sense to worry about it now? If you follow the IYD process, you will actually build a safety net as you go along with the program. We'll show you how to handle emergencies on a cash basis, even if you have no safety net. In the meantime, we say stop worrying about the six-month safety net and start working towards the biggest safety net possible by first investing in your debt!

Even though we can demonstrate mathematically how you get a much better return when you invest in your debt than you can get with a safety net, some people still are uncomfortable cashing in their safety net. Students in our workshops may say "Oh I wouldn't be able to sleep at night if I cashed in my $5000 safety net!"

In response to those people we say one simple thing: "Then don't cash in your safety net!" This isn't a sleep deprivation program – it is a debt investing program. Figuring out how to best apply IYD in your life is all about choices. If you don't want to cash in all $5000 of your safety net, then just cash in $4000, or $2000, or whatever you are comfortable with. But recognize IYD is an investment – the more you invest and the sooner you do it, the sooner you will reach your goal.

Spend Smart Factor Finder Method # 4 – Restructure, but still Invest in Your Debt

Now this is a tricky one. We've all heard about debt consolidation loans. You know the ads, "save money by consolidating your debt." The concept is to take your high interest debt and consolidate it into lower interest debt. The desired end result is to decrease the minimum monthly payments required.

If you haven't consolidated your debt, you probably know someone who has. They perhaps pay off their credit cards or car loans by getting a new mortgage or a home equity loan that includes cash to pay those other debts. Conventional wisdom says this is good because they have lowered their interest rates.

While it's true they have lowered the interest rate, the Rest of the Story is that when people decrease their payments, what they are also doing is stretching out the time and total amount of money it will take to pay their debt back. Unfortunately for most people, when they use debt consolidation loans, they actually end up digging a deeper financial hole for themselves. But it gets even worse.

When people consolidate their debt, all of a sudden they feel like they have gotten a raise or "found" some extra money. What do we usually do in such cases? We spend the money! In fact many times people not only spend the money, but they add more debt. And you already know that will only take you further from true financial freedom.

Many people have already applied this concept in their life. They have consolidated their debt and lowered their payments so now they have more money available in their monthly budgets. But usually in a year or two, they have run up credit card balances again and probably have a new car payment. So while it may seem like a good idea on the surface, unfortunately for most people, when they use debt consolidation loans, they actually end up digging a deeper financial hole for themselves.

Debt consolidation by itself does not work. But when you combine debt consolidation with the proper education and the desire to invest in your debt, then you are restructuring your debt.

The only way debt consolidation can work is if you use the money you save on minimum monthly payments and add it to your Spend Smart Factor.

If our typical family decided to restructure their debt, how would this affect their IYD program? When they start the IYD program, they have a total of $169,341 in debt with minimum payments of $1964. Let's assume they want to restructure their credit card and car debts into an additional home equity loan. These debts total $27,813 with monthly payments of $818. If they get a home equity loan at the same 10.11% rate that they have on their other home equity loan, the second equity loan would have a monthly payment of $301. This means they would now have an extra $517 in their monthly budget because their minimum payments are decreased by $517!

Again that seems great, but in order to restructure debt, you must take the money you save on payments with debt consolidation and use it for your Spend Smart Factor. Since the $517 is larger than the 10% Spend Smart Factor (our typical family's 10% Spend Smart Factor is $427), one would assume that they can eliminate their debt faster just by restructuring. However, this is usually not the case because you must look at the total amount that someone is investing in their debt each month.

One of the reasons someone would consider restructuring their debt is if there is absolutely no way they can come up with any extra money to invest in their debt. That is, most people who consider restructuring have a Spend Smart Factor of $0. Restructuring is the only way the can create a Spend Smart Factor so their total monthly investment in remains at the $1964 it was before restructuring. If our typical family does find a $427 (10%)

Spend Smart Factor, this gets added to the $1964 they are currently investing in their debt for a monthly total of $2391.

Please be cautious with this concept of restructuring. When our typical family restructures as described above, if they use the $517 as the Spend Smart Factor and invest it in their debt, it takes them eight years and 10 months to eliminate their debt. This is much better than the 10 years and eight months it takes to eliminate their debt if they have a Spend Smart Factor of 0%. In both cases, their total monthly debt payment remains at $1964. Restructuring allows the debt to be eliminated faster, because the total payment of $1964 is $517 more than the required minimum payment.

The Spendsmart family can still get out of debt faster without restructuring if they can just find a 10% Spend Smart Factor. So why would someone consider restructuring their debt? There are a number of specific circumstances where someone should consider restructuring.

One case would be when people are starting to have trouble making minimum payments. Perhaps they are even taking cash advances from credit cards to make other payments. Another case might be where their monthly budget is so tight, where they might even be going into the hole a little each month, and they cannot find any Spend Smart Factor Of course, if they want to get out of debt in seven years and 11 months, the time it would take with a $427 Spend Smart Factor without debt consolidation, restructuring their debt can still help. If they can find just an additional Spend Smart Factor of $183 and add it to the $517 they get from restructuring, and begin investing this total of $700 in their debt, they will be debt free in seven years and 11 months.

There are many variables that determine whether restructuring can assist someone with their IYD program. These variables include interest rates, payments and terms of course, but they also include the number of debts, the structure of debts and their relationship to each other. Debt restructuring is like nuclear power. Handled with great care, and in a proper manner, it can provide the power you need to invest in your debt. But you only get one chance to do it right. Make a mistake, and the radioactivity of debt consolidation will kill your financial future!

WE STRONGLY SUGGEST YOU CONSULT WITH YOUR SEMINAR LEADER TO DETERMINE IF DEBT RESTRUCTURING IS SOMETHING YOU SHOULD CONSIDER!

Your seminar leader can provide you with a complimentary computer analysis to help you determine if such an approach makes sense for you Do not rely on traditional advisors as your only source of information regarding debt consolidation. Most do not understand the power of investing in your debt. They only know what conventional wisdom tells them. And you know where conventional wisdom will get you!

Debt consolidation can help people in very specific circumstances if they commit to debt restructuring. If you simply want to lower your payments, don't bother because you will only devastate your financial future as many have already unfortunately done. But if you want to use debt restructuring to help you invest in your debt, in the right situation, with the right education and guidance, it can be of great benefit.

Spend Smart Factor Finder Method # 5 – Resist the Wealth Worms!

No, we're not talking about that bunch of spies! The worms we are talking about are like worms inside an apple. They eat away at the core of your current financial situation. Since they are below the surface, they are hard to see. The worst thing about the wealth worms is that they rob you of your wealth, slowly, over time, without you even realizing it! We call three of the wealth worms Easy Eddie, Pampered Patty and Appearance Annie.

These wealth worms are the reasons people buy things that they don't necessarily need. Please know we aren't against spending money or having fun. Life is a matter of choices. And now that you know how to invest in your debt, and you realize how much impact a few dollars here and there can have on your financial future, maybe you will want to make some different choices regarding the wealth worms. Let's look at these wealth worms a little more closely.

EASY EDDIE – Easy Eddie wants you to do things that save you time or makes your life easier. Grabbing lunch at the fast food restaurant is a good example of Easy Eddie. You could make lunch and bring it to work, but hitting the drive-thru is so much easier!

The typical worker spends $100 each month eating out for lunch.[5] But it's your choice – you can eat out at lunch, or you can brown bag it just once a week and invest the money you save. Over our working lifetime (40 years), eating out one day less a week allows you to accumulate an additional $126,482 of wealth. Which would you rather have – one extra burger and fries each week, or an extra $126,482 of wealth at retirement?

PAMPERED PATTY – Pampered Patty likes to indulge in only the finest things. Sometimes it is important to pamper yourself to recharge your batteries and relax. A good example is "designer" ice cream. You know what we are talking about – the stuff made from pure cream and lots of sugar. The stuff that has more fat grams in a pint than most people get in all other foods in a whole day!

It's okay to pamper ourselves, but what about all the different "designer" stuff we may consume in the food and refreshment area. Specialty coffee, microbrew beer, imported chocolate, etc. Do you think you could choose to look at the things you indulge in and find maybe $20 a month that you could save on spending and still find ways to pamper yourself a little? That $20 each month helps our typical family get out of debt two months sooner. It also allows them to build $33,774 more in wealth than they could without a Spend Smart Factor in the same time they would have normally just been struggling to pay off their mortgage.

APPEARANCE ANNIE – Appearance Annie loves to, as the cliché says, "keep up with the Joneses." She wants to have nice stuff and sometimes measures herself by comparing her stuff to her neighbor's stuff. So if her neighbors have nice new cars in the driveway every two years, it can be

---

5 John Cummuta, *Debt-FREE & Prosperous Living*, 8th ed. (Boscobel, WI:Debt-FREE & Prosperous Living, Inc., 1998)

tempting to want to do the same. You don't want to hold down property values in the neighborhood, do you?

Many people today always have a car or car lease payment because Appearance Annie wants them to "look good." People who lease cars are doomed to have car lease payments forever unless they make a drastic change. What if you make a choice to buy your vehicles, and keep them for twice the period you make payments on them? If you make payments on a car for three years you would then commit to keeping the car for twice that amount of time, or six years. That means half of your lifetime you would have a car payment and half of the time you would not.

What could you do with that extra money? Half of the time, you would have an extra $330 (average car payment). You can invest that money into traditional investments during those years you don't have a car payment and build quite a nest egg. In fact, you can choose to make $330 car payments forever or you can choose to only make payments for half of your working lifetime and build a nest egg so large that you earn over $6000 each month in income from it. So ask yourself, would you rather keep up with the Joneses and have a new car every few years, or would you rather have an additional $6000 in monthly income at retirement?

Examine the wealth worms in your life. Each time you are buying something, ask yourself if Easy Eddie, Pampered Patty or Appearance Annie is influencing your purchase. Again, what you do is your choice. But now you have a better understanding of how seemingly small financial choices can have a huge impact on your long-term financial health!

Spend Smart Factor Finder Method # 6 – Throw out your Credit Cards!

This topic is covered in great deal in the What the Credit Cards Hope You Never Find Out chapter, but we need to touch on it here because credit cards can have a huge impact on your Spend Smart Factor, even if you pay them off each month! Now don't get nervous about giving up the beloved credit cards – we will show you how to live on a cash basis even when emergencies strike – you won't need credit cards! Let's simply look at how getting rid of credit cards increases your Spend Smart Factor.

We all know that when someone uses a credit card, they spend more money than they would if they used cash. You know what we mean. When you slap down the plastic, **it just doesn't feel like money!** If you had a choice of walking into your favorite store with just cash or just a credit card, in which situation do you think you would spend more money? With the credit card of course! We all know this intuitively.

So how much more money do people tend to spend when they use credit cards instead of cash? Studies have shown that people will spend up to twice as much when they use credit cards. The bottom line is you will spend less money when you use cash. Cash is self-policing.

So how much money can you save each month by using cash? It depends on how much you currently use your credit cards. Based on the average credit card balance of $8000, the typical family probably spends at least $200 - $300 on credit cards each month.

Does the average family spend twice as much with credit cards as they would with cash? Probably not. What if the average family is fairly disciplined and they only spend 25% more than they would with cash? 25% of $200 a month is $50 each month. And this doesn't include the interest savings. Would you agree, based on what you know from personal experience that this is probably a low estimate?

Because you are reading this book, we assume you will stop using your credit cards. The question is how much does this add to your Spend Smart Factor? Take a look at your recent credit card statements. What are the average monthly spending amounts? Do you think you are spending 10%, 20%, 50% or more extra when you use your credit cards?

Figure out how much you will save by getting rid of your credit cards. This is money that goes right to your Spend Smart Factor. Stop using credit cards, even if you pay them off each month, and you will have more money to invest in your debt!

Spend Smart Factor Finder Method # 7 – Spending Review

As humans, we are creatures of habit. We get comfortable doing things in a certain way. This comfort can lead to inertia or a resistance to change. This resistance to change is not always bad. For example, one thing we definitely want you to get comfortable with is investing in your debt!

Sometimes however, we get comfortable with spending habits that are not helpful to the goal of achieving true financial freedom. When habits are formed, we tend to forget about them and they become automatic. There are many ways you can increase your Spend Smart Factor by slightly changing some habits. But you need to review your spending habits in order to recognize which habits may be worth less than true financial freedom.

Again, it is a choice. Use the Spend Smart Factor Spending Review Form found in Appendix A6. Review your choices you make in different spending areas. Make some decisions. Which spending habits do you want to continue and which are you willing to trade to help you invest in your debt and achieve true financial freedom.

Think about it. Do you really need all 200 cable channels? Now that you have the ability to create financial freedom, what's the point of buying lottery tickets? Do you really have to dine out every night? (If you do, your clothing expenses will increase as your waistline does!) Are there ways you can save money in your current spending that won't make you feel like you are depriving yourself, but instead make you feel like you are taking positive steps towards achieving your financial goals and dreams?

The choice is yours, we won't tell you what to do. Just review the form on page A6 and see if you find anything that pales in importance to true financial freedom.

Spend Smart Factor Finder Method # 8 – Baby Steps

As you know, you can still follow the *Invest in Your Debt* program even if you have a Spend Smart Factor of 0%. You also know however that every dollar you can add to the amount you invest in your debt each month has a tremendous impact on the wealth you can build. Don't get overwhelmed by the amount of Spend Smart Factor you want to find. As Bill Murray learns in the movie *What about Bob?,* just take "baby steps!"

Based on what you've learned so far, do you think you could find $1 a day to add to your Spend Smart Factor? Sure you could! Do you think you could find $100 a day to add to your Spend Smart Factor? Probably not, though many people, once they have eliminated their debt will have a Spend Smart Factor of over $100/day! Somewhere between these two extremes of a $1 a day and $100 a day is your Spend Smart Factor. As little as $3 a day, times 30 days in a month will generate almost $100 of Spend Smart Factor money. Don't worry about where you are now, just start taking baby steps towards your Spend Smart Factor goal, one step at a time.

The mathematics of *Invest in Your Debt* is fascinating. For example, we know that if someone starts with a $100 Spend Smart Factor, and finds a way to increase that to $200, they will get out of debt faster and be able to create more wealth. Since they have doubled their Spend Smart Factor, does this mean they will be able to eliminate their debt twice as fast and build twice the amount of wealth? If you've paid attention to our typical family example, you know the answer is no.

Your Spend Smart Factor follows what is known in economics as the law of diminishing returns. Adding to your Spend Smart Factor does give a return – that is, it gets you out of debt faster and helps you build more wealth. But every additional dollar added to your Spend Smart Factor has slightly less impact than the dollar that preceded it.

How should the law of diminishing return impact your efforts to build a Spend Smart Factor? You need to recognize…

The first $100 of Spend Smart Factor money has the greatest impact on your IYD plan!

If you can find $100 of Spend Smart Factor money, this is the $100 each month that will have the biggest impact on your financial future. Now we are not saying stop at $100. But the second $100 of Spend Smart Factor money will not have as much impact as the first $100. Of course the second $100 has more impact than the third $100…

Do you get the idea here? Baby steps. Don't overwhelm yourself thinking "how am I going to find a $427 Spend Smart Factor?" Take the baby step of finding the first $100 and focus solely on that. Once you find that first $100 "seed money," then start looking for the second $100, and so forth.

The $100 you can find for your Spend Smart Factor is more important than the $100 you cannot find. Once you start seeing some debts get paid off, you will get excited. You will start finding ways to find Spend Smart Factor money that you would never have thought of previously.

Summary

In this chapter, we have provided you with a number of general approaches with which you can build your Spend Smart Factor. For some people, these general approaches will be enough to create the amount of Spend Smart Factor they want. Others will want more specific strategies for creating Spend Smart Factor money. For this reason, we created the Spend Smart workshop and textbook.

In Spend Smart, we help people learn hundreds of ways to save money on insurance, groceries, energy costs, auto expenses and more. But Spend Smart is more than just another book about "how to save money on spending." Everybody knows how to save money on spending. In fact, most people save money on spending every day. The important question however is "what happens to that money people save?" If they save $200 on spending in a month, does that mean they have an extra $200 cash at the end of month?

Knowing how to save money on spending is not enough, because knowledge alone does not put cash in your hand at the end of the month. Just as *Invest in Your Debt* provides the linear math / variable path process to turn debt into wealth, *Spend Smart* provides a process as well! In Spend Smart, the K+PAR process turns savings on spending into cash in your hand at the end of the month.

The K+PAR process includes Knowledge PLUS a Plan, an Action and a Review. It is loosely based on what millionaires do as described in the book *The Millionaire Next Door*. Let's look at the components of the K+PAR process:

KNOWLEDGE is all the ideas about how to save money without making drastic changes in your life. Everyone knows you can save money if you change your own oil in your car. It also takes a good deal of effort to change your own oil. If you want to do it, more power to you. But Spend Smart focuses more on ideas for saving money that require you to simply make a one-time change that continues to save money month after month. We prefer money-saving ideas that you can put on "auto-pilot" and forget. PLAN is a budget. But don't worry, this isn't like a traditional budget that most people hate and never keep updated anyway. In Spend Smart, we have developed a unique "Reverse Budget." With a Reverse Budget you don't track every dime of spending. In fact, you track no spending at all. The Reverse Budget tracks savings. It only is used as a plan for the specific things you will do to save money and to track how much money you will save.

ACTION has two components. The first action is to apply your Spend Smart knowledge and save money. The second action is to seize your savings and turn them into cash at the end of the month. This action makes sure that the money you save doesn't disappear into other spending.

REVIEW is needed to keep your PLAN up to date. Spend a few minutes each month and decide what Spend Smart knowledge and action is working for you, what is not, and make appropriate changes. Like IYD, Spend Smart is flexible and can be adapted to the real world situations that arise on the road to true financial freedom.

For people who are serious about being successful with *Invest in Your Debt*, attending a Spend Smart class and/or getting a copy of the home study course will greatly increase your chances of success. In *Spend Smart* you learn that true financial freedom is a choice. We hope you choose to Spend Smart!

Chapter 4

Living on a Cash Basis!

People of all economic and income levels attend our workshops and seminars. Whether someone makes $12,000 a year or $120,000 a year, our experience shows that these people all have a number of characteristics in common. One notable characteristic is that they often spend money they don't have.

Remember when you were a kid and you would see an ad for some new toy? There were always so many things you thought you desperately needed, but unfortunately your parents often didn't see things the same way. As a parent, we put off the kids by saying "wait until your birthday" or "maybe Santa will bring it."

Eventually these kids who want everything become adults who have their own money and make their own choices. As an adult, have you ever wanted something, but didn't have the money in your checkbook to buy it now? It seems when that happens all those memories of being denied as a kid come rushing back. Your brain screams at you "I want it, I want it!!!" And I want it NOW!

The adult voice inside your head reminds you that if you really want this item badly, you can wait a little while until you saved up the money to buy it. But the kid's voice in your mind starts to justify other choices. You work hard, and you deserve to treat yourself every now and then, don't you? Besides, our friends at the credit card companies make it easy to not wait.

When we want something, it is all too easy for us to get it now, even if we don't have the money, because we can use credit to "buy now and pay later." Why wait when you don't have to? Since it is easy to not wait, most of us don't. We want it now and we get it now.

Psychologists call this phenomenon the **inability to delay gratification**. We use a less formal term. When you absolutely, positively must have something now, we call that the **"Gimmies."**

Are you familiar with the Gimmies? Any of us with children probably can relate. You know… "Gimmie this" and "Gimmie that." I want it now and I won't take no for an answer!

It doesn't take a rocket scientist to understand the first rule of debt elimination.

If you want to eliminate your debt, you must STOP CREATING NEW DEBT!

If you are in a leaking rowboat, and water is coming in faster than you can bail it out, YOU WILL SINK! The same applies to creating debt. Now we understand that this seems almost un-capitalist to say no more credit purchases, but follow our thought process here…

To stop creating new debt, you must LIVE ON A CASH BASIS!

We include checks and debit cards in our definition of cash. To live on a cash basis you need to be able to avoid the "Gimmies" so you don't buy things you don't need. So therefore…

If you ever want to achieve true financial freedom by investing in your debt, the FIRST STEP is to begin living on a cash basis.

Think of your financial life like a bucket. You pour money into it each month like water. Now there are some holes in the bucket. Each hole represents an expense. The larger the expense, the larger the hole, the more money that pours out of the hole each month.

When you create a new debt, you punch another hole in your financial bucket. If you add to an existing debt, you make that hole larger.

Until you start plugging some holes in your financial life, your financial future will continue to drain away.

To plug financial holes, to stop creating new debt, you need to live on a cash basis.

LIVING ON A CASH BASIS MEANS ALL PURCHASES ARE MADE WITH CASH!

Now for those of you that are creative thinkers, this doesn't mean it's okay to get a cash advance on your credit card and then buy something **because you're using cash**. What it does mean is we need to make some changes. The real key to living on a cash basis is to change our attitude about debt.

We know for many, the idea of only buying something when you have the money for it sounds impossible. One of the reasons it seems impossible is because LIFE HAPPENS. Financial surprises arise. People understand why they need to stop creating new debt, but there are a bunch of "what ifs." We typically hear questions like this:

"What if the washing machine breaks down?"

"What if the car needs new brakes?"

"What if we need a new car?"

We all have financial surprises in our lives. Remember though, the *Invest in Your Debt* program is a flexible process. If you want to achieve true financial freedom, you need to be flexible enough to adapt your life to this process. At the same time however, the program needs to be flexible enough to adapt to the financial surprises that come up in your life. AND IT DOES!

It's easy to live on a cash basis when everything happens as planned. But how can you avoid using credit when financial surprises happen? An important part of this process is to…

PLAN ON FINANCIAL SURPRISES!

Please remember that 80% of what we worry about never happens. At the same time, some of our worries do occur. Rather than being surprised or unprepared for financial surprises, why not assume some will occur. If you expect some financial surprises will happen, you can prepare for them. To prepare for financial surprises, you simply need a plan. The good news is there is a simple plan to deal with financial surprises.

The best way to handle financial surprises is to have a modest (small) cash cushion.

Well of course! But how do you get a cash cushion? Think about typical household financial surprises. Things like an appliance breaking down or problems cropping up with the car (especially if you make the commitment to speed your IYD program by buying only a two to three year-old car as we recommend in the *Spend Smart* book). A doctor or dentist bill might suddenly appear. And of course, kids always need something for school, or dance class or basketball, etc., but they wait until the last minute to tell you. Would you agree that…

Most financial surprises can be handled for $500 or less!

If you need to buy a new washing machine, you can get a good one for less than $500. The brakes on your car can be fixed for $500 or less. Doctor or dentist bills are usually less than that. If you had $500 in cash, wouldn't that help you avoid using the credit cards (if you still have them)?

Many people use credit because they feel they don't have the cash for something they want or need. If you have $500 for "financial surprises," then you can handle most emergencies on a cash basis, wouldn't you agree? So the next question becomes, "Where do I get the $500 to handle financial surprises?"

Here's one of the beauties of the *Invest in Your Debt* program. IT ALREADY HAS A CASH CUSHION BUILT IN! If you start following this process, you will automatically be able to handle most "financial surprise" situations. But where is the cash cushion you ask?

Remember how the Spend Smart Factor accelerates the *Invest in Your Debt* program? Well the Spend Smart Factor can also be your cash cushion! Some people have a Spend Smart Factor of $500 or more, as soon as they begin the program because they find ways to find "extra money" in their spending habits. Others who can find little if any "extra money" have a Spend Smart Factor of $500 or more once they get a couple of debts paid off because the payments on those debts are now available to apply to other debts.

Most people following the IYD program can create a Spend Smart Factor of at least $500 in the first six months or less!

So how does the Spend Smart Factor work as a cash cushion? Remember, the Spend Smart Factor is EXTRA MONEY that you have created in your life. You could have created it in a number of ways. You might have found ways to save money on spending. It might come from the excess you had been paying above the minimum amounts on your debts. It also grows as debts are paid off and the payment for that debt is added to the Spend Smart Factor.

Since your Spend Smart Factor is extra money, or **money that you have choices with**, you can use it in a variety of ways. Of course, we suggest this money be invested in your number one priority debt. But if you are faced with a financial surprise one month, maybe you should choose to use the Spend Smart Factor money differently that month.

What we are saying is…

When you have a financial surprise, handle that surprise with cash from your Spend Smart Factor!

Let's say you are working hard to eliminate your debt. Then one month the brakes go out in your car. Prior to reading this book, how would most people typically pay for the brakes? CHARGE! CHARGE – the consumer mantra of the 90s is still going strong in the 21st century! Most people would use their credit card to pay for the brakes and create new debt.

Now however, you have the ability to handle financial surprises with cash. When surprises come, you simply take cash from your monthly Spend Smart Factor and pay for the surprise without using credit! In this way, you can continue your IYD program and stop creating new debt, even when emergencies arise.

Of course you will remember from our chapter on credit cards, that there ain't no such thing as a free lunch. There is a cost for using your Spend Smart Factor for something other than investing in your debt. The cost is it takes you a little longer to get out of debt (in this example it takes only one more month).

When you use your Spend Smart money for a financial surprise, you are in effect "taking a month off" from your IYD program. You aren't quitting the program. You haven't given up the program. You are simply making a choice, and that choice is this…

While using your Spend Smart money for financial surprises does delay your debt elimination process, it is far preferable to creating new debt when handling emergencies.

So if you have a financial surprise one month, and you use your Spend Smart money as your cash cushion, how much longer does it take for you to get out of debt? Well it depends on several factors. How long have you been investing in your debt? How many debts do you have remaining? How much of your Spend Smart Factor will you use as your cash cushion?

In general, when you "take a month off" from the program, it will take you a month longer to get out of debt. This isn't 100% accurate, but it is a solid estimate. To see with complete accuracy how using your Spend Smart Factor for an emergency impacts your debt freedom date, you need to make complex financial calculations.

The flexible nature of the IYD program will help you handle the financial surprises that life throws your way. In fact, it is actually much easier to handle financial surprises on a cash basis with a planned program than it is to do so without such a program. Part of the reason for this, is that (as you will learn in the chapter about credit card secrets) you always spend more when you use credit than when you use cash.

If you stop using credit, you will have more money, EVEN IF YOU BUY THE SAME THINGS YOU WOULD HAVE BOUGHT WITH CREDIT!

Think about that. It will be explained in detail in the next chapter. But all we've discussed so far is the "smaller" financial surprises. How can we continue to live on a cash basis when a big surprise comes along? Your $500 Spend Smart Factor will only get you so far. There are however, several ways you can handle larger financial surprises and still remain true to a cash basis lifestyle.

The further in advance you plan, the larger the financial surprise you can handle on a cash basis.

Sometimes you have the opportunity to plan in advance. For example, let's say you decide that you are going to move to another city, and you figure the moving expense will be about $1500. If you know this in advance, you can handle it with cash. In this example, you would simply keep your Spend Smart money for three months in order to accumulate the $1500 cash needed for the move. It would now take about three months longer to eliminate your debt, but that is much more favorable then creating new debt.

So you see it is possible to handle bigger expenses than one may have thought, as long as you plan ahead. But we recognize that this concept of spending only cash is a challenge to conventional wisdom. Usually in our classes someone will try to "stump the teacher" and ask "what if my car becomes completely useless, can no longer be driven and I must have a new car?"

This is an important topic because many people will need a different car at some point prior to the time they are debt free. Once you are debt free, buying a car for cash can be very easy because you now have all the money that used to be wasted on debt payments. But what can you do about buying a car before you are debt free? This is a tough situation, but never fear. Again, the IYD program is flexible enough to handle this large financial surprise.

The first step in handling the need for a new car is to analyze your situation and think about the real issues. Some of us get caught up with the idea that our car is a reflection of ourselves, a statement of prestige. Typically that notion will simply delay or prevent you from getting debt free. It's one of the choices folks. Which do you want more – an impressive car or true financial freedom?

Consider as well, what do most of us need a car for? Usually it is for getting to and from work. If your car is completely dead, and you absolutely must have a new car to get to work, first consider your definition of what is a "new car." (We address this issue in the chapter on automobiles in the *Spend Smart* book). We at IYD are big believers in buying a car that has the best value. Typically, once a car is two to three years old, it has depreciated 50%. This means you can often buy a two or three year-old car for half of what it sells for new. If the purpose of the car is to get you to and from work, does it really matter much if it is a 2006 model or a 2000 model?

Remembering that the less you spend on a car, (while you are trying to get out of debt) the sooner you will be financially free, you may want to consider the cheapest reliable car you can find. Typically, you can find a cheap but reliable car for $3000 to $5000.

You see, if you make the decision to get a car in this price range, it is not difficult to buy a car with cash. If you saved your Spend Smart Factor money for six months, you will have the cash to buy a reliable (though not pretty) used car. If the "death" of your current car surprised you though, if it was something you were not able to plan for, and then you probably can't wait six months for transportation to get you to work.

What are your options? What are your choices?

Could you walk or ride your bike to work while you are saving up for an inexpensive car? Maybe yes, maybe no depending on where you live…but what if you have a broken leg? Then you couldn't walk or ride a bike to work.

If you have a broken leg, could you ride the bus to work? It depends on whether there is bus service between your home and work…but what if you live way out in the country? Then you couldn't ride the bus.

So if you have a broken leg and you live way out in the country, what other alternatives do you have? Could you ask a co-worker or friend to car-pool? Maybe…but what if you have bad breath and none of your friends or co-workers like to be around you? Then you couldn't get a ride from them.

So if you have a broken leg, you live way out in the country and you have bad breath, do you have any other alternatives for getting to work? How about a relative? Could they help you get to work? But what if you're an orphan? Now what can you do?

The purpose of this little humor bit is to illustrate a point.

Whether you believe you can buy a car with cash or you believe you cannot buy a car with cash, you are probably right!

There are a million reasons why one cannot buy a car with cash. But for most people, if the desire for true financial freedom via debt freedom is strong enough, you can find a way to do what it takes to get there as quickly as possible. Remember, once you are debt free, buying a car will never again be a problem (because you will have all the old debt payment money as "extra" money going into your pocket each and every month). When you are debt free, your money truly is yours to do with as you choose!

We want to emphasize that a change in thinking is required to get debt free. Conventional wisdom says if you need a car, get a new one either with a loan, or even worse, with a lease! If we automatically assume the things conventional wisdom teaches us, however, the odds of achieving true financial freedom are stacked against us.

Back to our question, if you are trying to get out of debt, and your car dies, what do you do? Follow these steps…

1) Commit to buying a car with the best value – be willing to sacrifice appearance (remember how the wealth worms steal your wealth!) for true financial freedom.

2) Think creatively to see if there is anyway you can hold off buying another car until you can save enough Spend Smart money to buy it with cash.

If you are an orphan with bad breath and a broken leg who lives in the country and you still need a car to get to work but you've run out of all other options, then there is only one thing you can do…

3) GET A LOAN!!!!!

That's right, we advocates of debt elimination and investing in your debt are telling you to get a loan. We believe that debt itself is not the problem that is robbing people of their future wealth. It is keeping debt forever that is the thief, and making minimum payments that destroy people's financial future.

The *Invest in Your Debt* program recognizes that…

There are a small number of situations where you absolutely, positively have no choice other than to get a loan.

We don't see debt as the "devil." Debt is neither inherently good nor bad. What we do with debt, however, can be good or bad for our financial futures. There are rare situations where there may be no choice but to get a loan. These situations might include such instances as…

- When you have no other choice than to buy a different car
- Large, emergency medical costs
- Back taxes
- Educational expenses
- Buying a house (your first house only)

What we are against is the kind of routine, consumer-mentality debt that has put so many people on the brink of disaster. If you are absolutely committed to achieving true financial freedom by investing in your debt we feel confident that you can make the proper decision if you ever find yourself in a situation such as those described above. However, remember that 80% of what we worry about never happens so these things will probably never happen to you.

If you need to get a loan, then go ahead and do it! Now that you have been educated about investing in your debt, however, we suggest you do some things that conventional wisdom would not have suggested.

1. Get the loan from a relative or friend, not a financial institution if possible. Since many people who are beginning this program are stretched to their credit limit, a loan from a bank may be expensive or difficult to obtain. But if you really are an orphan with bad breath, then make sure you get the best value if you get a loan from a bank.

2. Once you have the loan, plug it into the IYD program. See where it fits into your debt prioritization plan. Apply the linear math, variable path process to this new debt and have it paid off in 12 to 18 months instead of five years or more!

We must caution the readers at this point, not to jeopardize their future financial freedom by abusing the flexibility of the *Invest in Your Debt* program. While there are a few instances where you really have to get a loan, there are many other instances where people might be tempted to think they need a loan when they really don't. Though astute students will already recognize this, for the record, let's point out some instances where someone following the plan would not need a loan.

1. Vacation
2. Recreational Vehicle (boat, camper, snowmobile, etc.)
3. Christmas / Expensive Gifts
4. New Wardrobe
5. etc…

Your plan is not about never having fun or not being able to buy what you need. It is about choices. We assume if you are going to make the choice to achieve true financial freedom, that choice will be more important to you than buying more "stuff," at least until you are truly financially free.

Once you are truly financially free, you can choose to buy much more stuff than you ever could buy when you were in debt. Wouldn't you agree that it is much better to buy things with cash? When someone following a debt elimination plan is tempted to create debt, AND THEY WILL BE TEMPTED AT SOME POINT, one of the best ways to stay dedicated to a cash-basis is to look at debt from a different perspective.

You see there really is only one reason people create debt. People create debt because THEY CHOOSE TO SPEND MONEY THEY DON'T HAVE! A better way to put it is…

When people buy something with credit, they are choosing to trade future income for something they want now!

Debt is a promise to pay for something at a later date. More importantly…

When people buy something with credit, they are also agreeing to pay much more for an item than they would if they paid cash.

Intuitively we all know this is true. The cost of most items purchased on credit will include interest costs. If the cost of an item includes interest costs, obviously that is greater than the cost of the item itself. So why do people still choose to use credit when it costs more? We use credit because we are seduced by the grand illusion of credit.

We have been bombarded by advertising and marketing over the last few decades by the credit industry. The message of this marketing is simple – why wait to get what you want when you can have it now with credit? This message implies that credit helps us get what we want and therefore can improve our standard of living. For example, most people would think that someone who drives a new SUV probably has a higher standard of living than someone who drives a used compact car.

The idea that credit improves your standard of living is a grand illusion!

You can get many things sooner with credit than you would be able to get them with cash. That is true. As you might expect however, you need to become aware of the "rest of the story."

When you use credit, you are committing a portion of your future monthly income to debt payments. The more items you purchase on credit, the greater the portion of your future monthly income that is committed to debt payments. This means a smaller portion of your future monthly income will be available for things other than debt payments.

As your total debt payments increase, your ability to purchase other items actually decreases!

In other words, yes you can get something sooner if you use credit than if you wait until you have the cash. But you will recall the wisdom of the world – **there ain't no such thing as a free lunch** – there is a price to pay for being impatient and buying things with credit. That price is an increasing inability to purchase new stuff, because a growing amount of your income is already committed to paying for the old stuff, plus the interest! If you are less able to purchase new stuff because of increasing debt payments, isn't it fair to say…

Using credit actually decreases your standard of living!

So if using credit actually decreases one's standard of living, how can we acquire stuff we need without damaging our financial future? This chapter comes full circle at this point.

The best way to purchase what you need while protecting your financial future is to live on a CASH BASIS!

For those of us who have been hooked on the ease of credit for years, the idea of living on a cash basis can be overwhelming. We might think it will be impossible. We have to change our thinking on this in order to be successful with our program.

For most of us, the reason it is difficult to live on a cash basis is that we have not been living on a cash basis!

Because we have been using credit, we increase the amount of our monthly budget that has been committed to debt payments. This decreases the amount of money we have available to buy things with cash. As our available cash decreases, we have less margin for error financially. When a financial surprise "hits us between the eyes," we don't have the cash to handle it. Hence, we need to use more credit. Can you see why we say…

The more credit we use, the more credit we need!

It is a vicious cycle. When you think about it, isn't credit a lot like drugs or alcohol? At first you might just be a "recreational user." And many people never become more than that. But credit is so easy to get and use plus it provides immediate gratification. When you buy something, it feels good, doesn't it? If you like that feeling, and you want more of it, you may run out of cash. Using credit allows people to continue the "high" or good feeling one gets when buying things. It should surprise no one that people can actually get addicted to credit!

There is only one way to avoid this vicious cycle. That is to begin living on a cash basis. You can do it if you decide that your financial freedom is more important than "stuff." When financial surprises come up, use your Spend Smart Factor money to handle them.

It is much easier to live on a cash basis when you are debt free. At the same time, to get debt free, you need to live on a cash basis. Solving this apparent oxymoron or overcoming this "catch-22" is your toughest challenge when trying to achieve true financial freedom. Having taught this program to hundreds of thousands of people, our experience tells us that…

It is much easier to live on a cash basis if you have some cash!

While that may sound a little funny, it leads us to a suggestion that you may choose to consider. As we described earlier in this chapter, you can use your Spend Smart Factor as a cash cushion. If you have an emergency, this cushion is there to help you avoid using credit and to avoid damaging your financial future. But why not take this idea of having an emergency fund, one step further?

The key to achieving true financial freedom by first investing in your debt is to change habits, to make different choices than you had in the past. We have seen that one of the toughest challenges is living on a cash basis. The biggest reason this is so difficult is because it is a major change in the way people handle their financial lives.

To live on a cash basis, we are basically suggesting that when you have a financial surprise, you need to find the money to handle the surprise rather than creating more debt. You already know that extra money exists in your Spend Smart Factor, but that is not always the same as having the money available, when you need it, to avoid creating new debt.

For this reason, we suggest that some people may need to begin this program by first creating a small cash cushion of $200, $500 or even as much as $1000. This money should be put someplace where it won't be spent, unless there is a financial surprise. Where will this $200 - $1000 come from? It comes from your Spend Smart Factor of course!

One way to create this $200 to $1000 cushion is to pay just your minimum debt payments for a couple of months and keep your monthly Spend Smart Factor for the cash cushion. That way, since your program is realistic and plans on financial surprises, you will have the cash available immediately to handle such a surprise. You will no longer need to reach for the credit cards to handle an emergency. Like all other choices however, you need to consider the price you pay for creating this cash cushion.

Because you are using your Spend Smart money to build the cash cushion, you are not investing quite as much in your debt as you could be. If you use two months of Spend Smart Factor money, you will delay your debt freedom date by about two months. For our typical family, if they create a cash cushion of $1000, it will take them about two months to do so. This means it will take them two months longer to get out of debt. So instead of being out of debt in seven years and 11 months, they will be out of debt in eight years and one month.

If it takes our typical family eight years and one month to get out of debt, that's still much better than paying on their debt for 28 years and one month as conventional wisdom would teach, isn't it? At the same time, that two-month delay in debt freedom means the Spendsmarts will not have as much time for traditional investing. You will recall from the Linear Math chapter, that if our typical family invests the money they had been wasting on debt payments for 20 years and two months (the time they save on debt payments) they can build $1,850,840 of wealth in the same time they would have just been struggling to pay off their mortgage.

If our typical family chooses to use their Spend Smart Factor to build a small cash cushion, and it takes them two months longer to get out of debt, that means they will have two months less time to invest. When they invest their debt payments for just 20 years, they still build $1,815,651 in wealth. But notice, this is $35,819 less in wealth they are able to build when they choose not to create a cash cushion. The $1000 cash cushion costs them $35,819 of future wealth. For some however, the security of a small cash cushion may make it a choice worth making.

We believe it is important to focus on reality. Numbers such as those above are just projections, meaning they assume a perfect world. Since we know our financial worlds are not perfect, we think the most important aspect regarding a cash cushion is for you to do whatever makes you most comfortable.

If you are concerned that you will never be able to complete the *Invest in Your Debt* program unless you have a cash cushion, then you should build a cash cushion. If you feel confident that you can use your Spend Smart Factor to handle financial surprises, then don't build a cash cushion. The bottom line is if you feel you would be more comfortable knowing you have a cash cushion available, use your Spend Smart Factor to create one!

If you decide to create a cash cushion, the next question is when is the best time to do it? The answer to this question varies greatly depending on individual circumstances. If the comfort of having a cash cushion is of high priority to you, then you should create a cushion right away. If you feel you can wait a few months, it is easier to create the cash cushion once you have paid off your first debt.

SUMMARY

Just as we cannot save a sinking boat if water is leaking in faster than we bail it out, you cannot invest in your debt while you are still creating new debt. This concept is easy to understand. If you want to be successful with the *Invest in Your Debt* program, you must also stop creating new debt. And there is only one way to stop creating new debt. That is to begin living on a cash basis.

Address your situation from a realistic perspective as well. Some people are more comfortable with the idea that they won't use credit any more if they have a cash cushion. Some people feel more comfortable knowing that it's okay to get a loan, if you absolutely have to. If you do get a loan, just plug it into the process and pay it off in a matter of months instead of years.

Invest in Your Debt is a flexible process. One of the most important components is living on a cash basis. This is a choice and a decision. Before you read this book you probably would have thought you were making a choice between using cash or using credit. We hope that now you understand it really is a choice between achieving true financial freedom in a few years or laboring through a lifetime of financial hardship.

Chapter 5

Advanced IYD Strategies

We continue to emphasize that the *Invest in Your Debt* process is flexible. This is so important. We want the strategy and process to adapt to the surprises that real life brings us. IYD needs to adapt to what people are comfortable with. We don't care if you follow our concepts exactly. In fact, we don't even care if you follow conventional wisdom, as long as you achieve true financial freedom. Unfortunately, as you know, conventional wisdom leads to a life of financial struggle for most people.

We know that if you continue with the plan, you may experience some ups and downs, but we also know that you will eventually achieve your dreams, much faster than you ever imagined. It may take a few years longer than our typical family example, or it may happen faster if you really get excited and motivated.

HOW people achieve success with this program is not nearly as important as whether they stick with it or not.

Now that you understand the basics of the *Invest in Your Debt* program, there are a number of "twists" you might want to add to your plan, to make it even more realistic for you. Some of these "advanced strategies" get you out of debt faster while some slow the process.

Please bear in mind that not all of these strategies will appeal to everyone. Whether they make sense for you is your personal choice. But for the person who is dedicated to achieving true financial freedom, by first investing in their debt, these strategies provide more options for customizing the IYD plan to your specific circumstances.

Advanced IYD Strategy # 1: Alternative Debt Priorities

In the *Invest in Your Debt* program, we teach people to pay their debts in order from lowest balance to highest balance. This is what we call prioritization. Prioritization is deciding which debt to focus on first, which to focus on second, and so forth.

We teach this method of prioritization for a number of reasons, the least of which is not that it is the easiest to understand, plus it works! But there are other ways you can prioritize your debt. The fact that there are different ways you can prioritize your debt is in fact why we refer to the process as a "variable path" process. Some of the paths, or methods of assigning priority, will get you out of debt a little sooner while some take a little longer. Let's look at some of these alternative methods.

A question we are often asked in class, is "Why don't we pay the debt with the highest interest rate first?" Conventional wisdom, what we have always heard and been told, would tell us it makes sense to pay the highest interest rate first. The general reason is we don't trust our financial future to conventional wisdom. The truth is however in most cases, the prioritization method you use doesn't make much more than a month or two difference in when you will be debt free.

Now of course, there are prioritization methods that may make you feel good, but don't make much sense in terms of their financial outcome. For example what if you become so outraged by the fact that you will pay twice as much for the interest on your mortgage as you will pay for your house, that you decide no matter what, you will pay off your mortgage first. You might feel better about your plan, but it would take much longer to pay off your debt and you would build less wealth.

The best prioritization method is the one that works best for you. Different prioritization methods are better for different sets of circumstances. But even if there is a prioritization method that technically works best for you, what's more important is choosing the method that you feel comfortable with, that you will stick with! It's not nearly as important how you begin your road to true financial freedom as long as you start the journey by achieving debt freedom!

Advanced IYD Strategy # 2: Celebrate!

This is an advanced strategy that we believe everyone should use because it increases your chances of success! Anything you can do to make it more likely you will stick to the IYD program is something you should consider.

One of the potential challenges facing you on the road to financial freedom is the feeling that you are depriving yourself.

When you are working towards debt freedom, one of the ABSOLUTELY MANDATORY rules is that you should not create new debt. This of course means that you should live on a cash basis. In the past, when you used credit cards, you had the opportunity to buy most things you wanted, whenever you wanted them. Now that you will no longer use those "habit-forming, druggie" credit cards, you will not always be able to buy what you want, when you want. Now you know the reason for this is that you are making a choice. You are choosing true financial freedom over stuff.

Once you are debt free you can buy whatever you need whenever you need it. While you are working towards that goal, you may still occasionally feel deprived. It can be tempting to buy something on credit, even though you know buying on credit is just an illusion for paying much more for something that eventually costs you cash when you pay the credit card bill. In order to help you fight the feelings of depriving yourself that can come up during your IYD program, we think you should celebrate!

What does this mean? Think about the *Invest in Your Debt* process. When you get a debt paid off, what should you do with the money you had been paying on that debt? Well according to the process, you should take that money and "roll it up" to the next debt. When a debt gets paid off, you should add the payment you had been making to that debt to your next priority debt.

We think you should occasionally take a slightly different approach. When you pay off some debts, you should CELEBRATE! Take your Spend Smart Factor and the money you had been paying on that debt and CELEBRATE. Go have a great time!

For example, in just a little over a year, our typical American family will have paid off their first three debts. They will now have a total of $578 in "extra" money each month, including their Spend Smart Factor and the payments they had been making on debts that are now gone! Won't you want to celebrate when you start having extra money in your life each month?

Treat your family to a fun night out. Go to a show and a nice dinner. Spend a day at an amusement park. Go to a sporting event. Spend a weekend at a nice hotel. There are many things you can do. But here is the most important aspect of celebrating:

You can celebrate and pay for it with cash!

You have followed the IYD process for about a year. You have already gotten far ahead of where the typical family is in terms of their finances and debt. You deserve to pat yourself on the back and celebrate. The IYD program is not about depriving yourself and never having fun. It's not about scrimping and scraping pennies. The IYD process is about having fun while achieving true financial freedom. We know you need to celebrate, because…

You had fun getting into debt, didn't you? You therefore need to have fun getting out of debt as well!

So what we are advocating here is that you set some goals regarding the debt elimination process of your IYD program and reward yourself when you reach them. Get your family involved on what the goals and rewards should be. This involvement will pay off because they will be more supportive of your efforts to achieve true financial freedom by first investing in your debt. When you achieve your goal, pay for the celebration with cash by using your Spend Smart Factor.

Now of course this means that during those months that you celebrate, you will be taking a "vacation" from investing in your debt. If you celebrate one month, you will pay cash for the celebration and, therefore, only be able to make minimum debt payments that month. As you know, there is a price for taking a one-month vacation from IYD – that price is it will take you one more month to reach debt freedom. But we know that setting goals and rewarding yourself with a celebration paid for in cash is a good method for insuring you will stick with your plan.

So people might choose to celebrate one or two times on their way to having just their mortgage left to eliminate. Once you have paid off everything but the mortgage, you might want to consider a BIG CELEBRATION. You are about to attack the mortgage, the big beast that will choke the life out of your financial future if you let it. You need courage and determination to take that next step.

Those who attend our seminars tell us that one of the best ways to recharge their batteries, and build determination to make their goals, is to take a vacation. So maybe you should think about taking a vacation after you have paid off all your debt other than your first mortgage. But let's think big here. Once you have just your first mortgage left, you have completed a huge step in your journey to true financial freedom. Why not go for a huge reward as well?

Do you have a dream vacation? You know, a vacation you have always dreamed about, but you haven't ever been able to afford to take it! Once our typical family has everything but their first mortgage paid, **they now have an extra $1634** in their lives every month. They could take a pretty good vacation for that amount of money and they could pay for it with cash!

But what about that dream vacation? Could you take a cruise for $1634? Could you go to Europe? Could you take the family to Disney World for $1634? Probably not. But let's assume the Disney World vacation is the dream. Could you take that vacation for cash and still complete your IYD plan? The answer is yes!

If you plan ahead, and shop around for airfare, hotels, etc., you can have a wonderful family vacation at Disney World for around $5000. How can our typical family get $5000 to pay for the vacation in cash? Well, if they take about three months vacation from the IYD process, once they have paid everything but their first mortgage, they would have about $5000 cash because they now have an extra $1634 each month! Yes, you can follow the IYD program and still go to Disney World or whatever your dream vacation might be!

Maybe a dream vacation isn't something that motivates you. The point is this. Pick a reward that really motivates you to get to the point where almost everything is paid off and just your first mortgage remains. Then pay for your reward with cash by taking a month or two off from the process and saving the extra money you now have (thanks to IYD) in your life.

Celebrating is part of the flexibility that allows people to customize the *Invest in Your Debt* plan to fit their individual situations. Of course, you must be a little cautious and not get carried away. If you celebrate too often or too big, you will never achieve debt freedom, the first step towards true financial freedom. But well chosen goals with well-chosen rewards will make sure that you have fun, and stick to your plan, therefore insuring a happy financial future!

Advanced IYD Strategy # 3: Lump Sum Payments

Sometimes we experience a financial windfall in our lives. These are times when all of a sudden we get some money that we never expected. Though this never happens as much as we like, these times might include a tax refund, an insurance settlement or an inheritance.

What do we typically do when we get a surprise lump sum of money? We spend it! The thinking is that "Well I wasn't counting on it so I don't have any specific thing I need to spend it on – why not go wild?" Surprise money in our life tends to get spent wildly because it feels like "free" money.

Consider an alternative, because chances are there will be at least one occasion during your journey to debt freedom where a lump sum of money will surprise you by showing up in your life. You already know that we will suggest that you invest that money in your debt. But you need to understand the mathematics behind this thinking.

With the *Invest in Your Debt* process, "sooner" is always better than "later,", but it is never too late!

Here's what we mean by this. Let's say you get a $1000 tax refund or rebate. If you choose to invest that money in your debt, it has a bigger impact now than it would if you get a $1000 tax refund next year. That makes sense doesn't it? This happens because you are giving compound interest more time to work for you and less time to work against you. Sooner is always better than later.

But let's take it a step further. Lump sums are better than payments over time. For example, $1000 now has a bigger impact than $100 a month for 10 months. That's because you have more money taking advantage of the time value of money. So if you have a choice to make in terms of getting a lump sum of money now, or getting it in payments over time, it may be more beneficial in terms of debt freedom to get the lump sum now, and invest it in your debt.

If you don't foresee any lump sums of money falling into your lap, don't worry about it. Chances are some will come along at some point during your IYD program. And whenever it does, it is never too late to take advantage of the power a lump sum has on the debt elimination portion of your IYD plan. For example, if our typical family gets **a $1000 lump sum at anytime** during their IYD process, it will allow them to eliminate their debt one month sooner and **build an extra $17,614 in wealth**. That's a pretty good return on the $1000!

The important point about lump sums is that they you will probably have some surprise money appear in your life. Before the IYD program, most people would probably just spend the money wildly. But now that you are educated, if you instead choose to invest a lump sum in your debt, you will make a big impact on your journey to true financial freedom!

Advanced IYD Strategy # 4: Teach It!

This is an advanced strategy that can dramatically impact your financial future, and it doesn't impact the mechanics of the IYD program at all. Now that you learned of this awesome tool for achieving true financial freedom, you are probably excited about it. The authors of this book, and the seminar leaders who teach workshops across the country got excited when they first learned about IYD as well. These people would all agree, that one of the reasons they are successful in applying IYD to their lives is because they teach it!

Now don't get nervous – we are not suggesting you need to start getting up in front of large groups of people and speaking like our teachers do (though if you are interested in doing that, we do need help on our mission so mention it to your seminar leader). We are suggesting that you simply share the ideas and concepts with your family and friends. In fact, if you want to greatly increase the odds that you will stick with the program, and therefore be successful with it...

IN THE NEXT 48 HOURS YOU NEED TO TEACH *INVEST IN YOUR DEBT* TO 2 OTHER PEOPLE!

Why would you want to teach IYD? We learn one of the best reasons from Stephen Covey is his famous book <u>The Seven Habits of Effective People</u>. Covey teaches that if you want to master a subject, learn it inside and out, to internalize it and truly make it your own, you need to TEACH IT! By teaching IYD, you will get to understand and learn the process more and therefore be better able to implement it in your life.

Teaching it to two other people is as simple as just telling them about the concept. Letting them know that they can be debt free in about 7 years, including their mortgage, using nothing more than the money they already bring home. You can also tell them that in only about 20 years, they can be millionaires – they can have a net worth of more than $1 million dollars. Again, to do this, they don't need to win the lottery, they don't need to get a raise or a second job, they don't need to start a business. To achieve true financial freedom, all you need to do is invest in your debt!

You can take it further. Sit down with these two people and walk them through the process with this textbook. Help them fill out the <u>What Should I Pay First?</u> form in Appendix A2. Help them determine when they can be out of debt by using the <u>Debt Free Date Calculator</u> form in Appendix A3. Get them really excited when you show them how to use the <u>When Will I Be a Millionaire</u> form in Appendix A4. We promise you, showing other people how IYD can change their lives is one of the most personally rewarding experiences you will ever have.

There is one final reason why you should teach IYD to (at least) 2 other people. Think about this – if you tell some of your friends about how you are working towards true financial freedom by first investing in your debt, what do you think will happen when you see them a month or two later? They will ask you "How are you doing with that *Invest in Your Debt* thing?"

By teaching others, you build accountability for yourself. You know that they will ask you about it later and you certainly don't want to tell them "Oh. I have slipped back into my old habits that are stealing true financial freedom from my family and I!" Teach *Invest in Your Debt* to others, and you will greatly enhance the chance that you will stick with the plan!

Summary

We call this chapter "Advanced Strategies" not because they are difficult. We call them advanced because we want you to first understand the process in its simplest form, as taught in the <u>Linear Math / Variable Path</u> chapter. Once you understand the basics, then you can add these strategies to your program. But don't let the word "advanced" scare you. Even if you are new to *Invest in Your Debt*, all of these strategies are really things anyone can do.

The purpose of having advanced strategies is to provide tools that you can use as part of "customizing" the IYD program to your specific situation. Customizing the program for yourself will increase the likelihood of you sticking to the program.

We know, and you do as well, that *Invest in Your Debt* works!

So the key to increasing your odds of success is completely based on increasing the likelihood of sticking to the program. We hope this chapter on Advanced Strategies helps you stick to it. It doesn't really matter how you implement the program, as long as you "just do it."

Chapter 6

What Credit Card Companies Hope You Never Find Out!

Have you ever had a craving for chocolate? Chocolate cravings are challenging in the inner battle they create between a person's head and their stomach. Your head says you probably shouldn't eat it…but your stomach reminds you it will taste soooo good!

See if this scene sounds familiar. You want chocolate, but you don't want the extra calories. But when you really think about it, what harm would a little taste do. You reassure yourself – "I have will power! I can have just a taste of chocolate, satisfy my craving, and I won't have any more!" So you take a little nibble of chocolate, and it tastes so good – oh that tastes good.

Now since you've already broken your diet, you may as well eat a little more. Pretty soon you've eaten half of the chocolate by nibbling. Perhaps you're feeling a little guilty. You tell yourself, "I don't want to eat any more chocolate." You also don't want to be tempted to eat more chocolate later, therefore, it makes perfect sense to finish eating all of the chocolate NOW – that way, you won't have to worry about it later.

This chapter is about credit cards, so it makes perfect sense to talk about chocolate, doesn't it? You see credit cards are a lot like chocolate. If you don't use your credit cards very often or eat too much chocolate, you'll probably be okay. But like chocolate, credit cards exist on a slippery slope. The more you use credit cards, the easier it is to use them again. If you eventually find yourself where you've overdone it with credit cards, you could spend a lifetime trying to pay them off just as you could spend a lifetime trying to work off the extra padding around your middle from chocolate.

Now we don't want to turn people off here – we're not saying everyone has or will get into trouble with credit cards. If you've never had the credit card blues, congratulations! Even if you've never fallen into the minimum payment we encourage you to study this chapter thoroughly anyway. Just like the analogy of fire, credit cards could still "burn you" one day if you aren't careful. Even if you pay them off each month!

One of our seminar leaders tells the story of when he got his first credit card – while in college of course – he was excited! Maybe you can relate to this story. It felt like someone had given him a bunch of money. He decided he and his friends were going to play "Cavalry" – you know, they ran all around town and yelled "CHARGE!"

One of the first things he learned was that the "green" card was so "exclusive" that it wasn't accepted everywhere. So when he treated his friends to dinner, he had to make sure the place they went was "sophisticated" enough to take his card. If they did not, then they certainly did not deserve his business since "membership has its privileges."

He and his friends lived high on the hog for about 30 days. But then, suddenly a dark cloud appeared over this free-spending lifestyle. THE CREDIT CARD BILL CAME IN THE MAIL! He was surprised when he saw the total. It didn't seem like that much money when he signed the receipts! And guess what…one of the "privileges of membership" was that the entire amount had to be paid in full each month.

As you can imagine, as a college student with little or no income, he was in trouble. Fortunately, he had the most vital financial resource any college student can ever have – Mom & Dad. They paid the bill and allowed him to pay them back. Nice of them, wasn't it? They only asked for one item in return – they got to keep his precious credit card until he had a job.

Now most of you reading this book probably were not as impulsive as he was as a college student, but do you remember when you got your first credit card? Did you buy some things right away, items that you didn't have the money for right then, but you felt you could afford the "low monthly payments?" Most of us have.

Perhaps there was a time when you decided your credit cards would only be used for emergencies. Your definition of emergency included items like surprise car repairs and such. Over time however, your definition of "emergency" evolves. After a while, a sale at the mall before payday qualified as an emergency. Perhaps eventually your definition of emergency could include "I want to go out for dinner and fun but my wallet says no!" Do you have any credit cards? Chances are you do since in the US alone there are over one billion credit cards in circulation.[6] ONE BILLION CREDIT CARDS! That's almost four credit cards for each man, woman and child. Now we assume that most of the 50 million grade school and younger children don't have credit cards, so…that means some of us have many more than four credit cards!

For many of us, credit cards have become a reflex, an automatic way we pay when we are shopping at certain stores or when we spend more than a certain dollar amount. You could say credit cards are a habit. Some habits are good and some are bad. As with any habit, it can be beneficial to "ask why" now and then. We hope, after reading this chapter, you will ask yourself "Why do I need credit cards?"

Most of us have probably never even questioned the reason why we have or use credit cards. They seem like a normal and necessary part of our financial lives. It's interesting when you consider however, that credit cards have really only been around since the mid 1960s. Then, when you saw someone using a credit card it was a novelty. It wasn't until the mid 1980s that credit cards really became prevalent. Now, credit cards are used so frequently, it's almost a novelty to see someone using cash!

There is one simple reason why most people accept and use credit cards so willingly. The credit industry has been very successful marketing their products to us. You've seen the commercials – "MasterCard – it's smart money." We are taught to think it is good financial strategy to use credit cards at the grocery store, because it allows us to "track our spending."

A big part of the successful credit card marketing has been the sheer volume and amount of it. Credit card companies are always big advertisers during big TV shows. And how about all that mail we get? Many of us get several

---

6 "Zero Balance-Getting the Credit Monkey Off Your Back", Family Money Magazine, July 2000

credit card offers a week. According to Consumer Reports, credit card advertising has been very successful in shaping our thinking. We've been told that credit cards help us enjoy life more, help us get the finer things in life. Credit cards are marketed as tools of the financially-savvy. We are led to believe that credit cards will somehow improve our financial lives when in reality…

Instead of helping us financially, credit cards actually rob typical families of the ability to achieve true financial freedom!

In other words, for most people…

If you use credit cards on a regular basis, you probably will never be able to retire!

Does this seem a little harsh? Let me put it to you in another way…

You have a choice. You can continue using credit cards or you can begin to build real wealth: wealth such that you can become financially free!

These statements seem a little preposterous, don't they? That's okay to admit it because most people in our classes don't believe it at first either. But it is absolutely true. For most people, **credit cards do nothing but drain their future wealth!**

LET US SHOW YOU HOW!!!!

As you learned earlier in this book, all that stands between true financial freedom and the typical family is an extra $427 (10% Spend Smart Factor) a month. We define financial freedom as $1,000,000 or more in net worth. As you read this chapter, you will learn that the typical family would have that extra $427 per month, if they would just break the credit card habit.

Without credit cards, the typical family would have an extra $427 per month. With that extra $427 a month, they can invest in their debt and THEY CAN ACHIEVE TRUE FINANCIAL FREEDOM!

According to CardWeb.com, a Frederick, Maryland firm specializing in on-line publication of credit card information, trends and statistics (formerly known as RAM Research), at the end of 1998, the average household owed $5751 on their credit cards.[7] Like other debt, credit card debt has risen in the last few years as well. Since CardWeb also tells us there are 79 million households with at least one credit card, and the Federal Reserve tells us that the total credit card debt (revolving debt) in the US is about $633 Billion,[8] we can use some simple math to determine that today's average credit card balance for the typical household is $8013.

Now for those who think, 8000 bucks, that's not too bad…consider a number of facts that keep this average lower than it might have been. First, refinancing mortgages and "consolidating debt" have been very popular (though they are often financial suicide) conventional financial tactics the last few years. When people consolidate, they often "pay off" their credit cards. Of course, that debt doesn't disappear; it just now is part of the mortgage. So it is reasonable to assume that credit card debt would be much higher were it not for the mortgage refinancing binge of the last few years.

Another factor that keeps the average credit card balance low is the fact that a number of people pay off their balances in full each month. When you include many people who pay their balance off each month, it makes the average balance seem lower for the people who do carry a balance. Further information from CardWeb tells us in fact that 42% of people pay their cards off each month.[9]

So if 42% of the 79 million households with credit cards pay them off each month, that means that 58%, or 46 million households carry credit card balances and don't pay them off each month. So if we want to know the average balances of those who carry a balance, we need to divide the total credit card balance ($633 Billion) by the total households carrying credit card balances.

---

[7] http://www.cardweb.com/cardtrak/pastissues/oct99.html
[8] http://www.federalreserve.gov/releases/g19/
[9] http://www.cardweb.com/cardtrak/pastissues/oct99.html

If you carry balances, and were thinking the $8000 average is low compared to your balances, maybe you will realize that you are closer to "normal" than you might have thought when you realize the average balance, <u>for those who carry credit card balances</u>, is actually $13,761!

With credit cards, most people are doomed to a lifelong merry-go-round ride of using credit cards, slowly paying them down, using credit cards, slowly paying them down. Credit cards are the fastest route to financial disaster.

The purpose of this chapter is not to lecture about the evils of credit cards, though the statistics speak for themselves. The purpose is not to convince people to cut up their credit cards (though you may choose to once you see how much wealth those credit cards are costing you). The purpose of our credit card discussion is to simply encourage you to re-examine your use of credit cards from a more educated perspective. Here's the "Rest of the Story."

First, let's look at how big the number of credit cards in circulation really is. Think about how much one billion is...

One billion days is 2,739,726 years
One billion hours is 114,155 years
One billion minutes is 1,902 years
One billion seconds is 32 years

A BILLION CREDIT CARDS IS A BUNCH OF CREDIT CARDS!

What do we do with all these credit cards? Well of course, we SPEND A LOT OF MONEY! According to CardWeb, credit card purchases topped $1 trillion in 1999.[10] As you'll soon learn, for most people, spending money with credit cards is the same as SPENDING MUCH MORE MONEY THAN YOU WOULD WITH CASH. For now, it's important to understand the scope of our credit card usage.

---

10 "Zero Balance-Getting the Credit Monkey Off Your Back", <u>Family Money Magazine</u>, July 2000

How much is a trillion? Well, it's simply a thousand times a billion. So you simply add three zeros to the end of the examples of a billion above and you learn that one trillion is…

One trillion days is 2,739,726,000 years (almost THREE BILLION Years!)
One trillion hours is 114,155,000 years
One trillion minutes is 1,902,000 years
One trillion seconds is 32,000 years

So a trillion dollars spent with credit cards is a lot of money. Some would say however…

"What does it matter how much is charged since most people pay off their credit card balances each month?"

Here is a chance for you to begin to see "the rest of the story."

According to the Federal Reserve, the outstanding balance on credit cards continues to rise each year, much faster than income rises. Typically, personal income grows about 2% each year. How does that compare to the growth of outstanding balances on our personal credit cards?

Look at the latest statistics about the total outstanding credit card balances and its growth from year to year…

Total Credit Card Balance

	1995	1996	1997	1998	1999	2000
$ Balance (Billions)	$443	$499	$531	$561	$596	$633
Balance % Growth	21%	13%	6%	6%	6%	12%

The growth in outstanding credit card balances had been slowing the last few years, but even 6% growth is high. What this means is that our outstanding balances are growing faster than our income. If balances are rising, can we not also assume that minimum payments are rising as well? It doesn't take a math whiz to realize…

When expenses (payments) grow faster than income this is a financial disaster waiting to happen!

Why do we have so many credit cards and use them so much? Maybe it's because credit cards are "smart money." Maybe it's because we can earn free travel and other "goodies" with the award programs. Maybe we like those cash back bonuses. Maybe we like the convenience. Maybe we like the prestige: didn't you think you were really special when you got your first gold card! Whatever we may think is the reason we have a wallet full of credit cards (that is, if we've ever stopped to think about it), there is one major factor that probably contributes to the large number of credit cards more than any other reason…

There are so many credit cards in circulation today…BECAUSE CREDIT CARD COMPANIES MAKE IT SO EASY TO GET THEM!

You've heard all the stories about dogs, cats, eight year old kids or deceased people being sent pre-approved credit cards in the mail. Obviously, those are mistakes, but there are many people who get credit cards that you would never imagine. People with bankruptcies and bad credit can easily get cards today. We'll talk more about these people later, but let's continue with the discussion of "Why do we have so many credit cards?" There is a deeper reason to consider.

Why do credit card companies make it so easy to get credit cards?

SIMPLY BECAUSE CREDIT CARDS ARE VERY PROFITABLE FOR THE CREDIT CARD COMPANIES!

It's a simple fact folks, the credit card industry is very profitable. We all think about Bill Gates as the richest man in the world, but do you know who the second richest American is? The fellow who owns MBNA, a credit card company that targets people with bad credit histories. Now you might wonder, how can one become wealthy by giving credit cards to bad credit risks?

MBNA does very well because their customers tend to be people who have no choices. That is, their customers typically can't get cards from other credit card companies. So, they are more likely to pay not only higher interest rates, but also higher fees and service charges. This leads us into…

Four Credit Card Company Secrets

1. Credit cards cost you money, <u>even if you pay them off each month!</u>
2. There ain't no such thing as a free lunch.
3. Minimum payments are designed to keep you in debt FOREVER!
4. Credit card companies that offer you a card when no one else will are not your friend!

Let's look at each of the secrets in detail.

1 – <u>Credit cards cost you money, even if you pay them off in full each month.</u>

People assume the only costs they need to worry about with credit cards are interest rates/charges and annual fees. They look for cards with no annual fees and an interest free grace period so they don't pay interest rates if they plan on paying off the card each month.

People often ask in our classes "I pay my credit cards off each month, so it's okay to use them, isn't it?" First let us repeat, our purpose is not to tell you what to do. But don't make the assumption that paying off your cards each month is the same as "having no cost." Yes, it is true that with most cards you won't pay interest charges if you pay your card off each month. There is however, a hidden cost most people fail to realize. Here's the rest of the story…

When you use a credit card you spend more money than when you use cash...

YOU SPEND MORE MONEY when you use a credit card. This truth is so obvious when you think about it. Let's say you need to get some clothes. You decide to go shopping at the local mall. Do you think you will spend more money if you go shopping with $100 cash or if you take your credit cards?

So even if you pay your bill off at the end of the month, you have less money left over at the end of the month because when you use your credit cards to make purchases you spend more than you would with cash. Therefore, CREDIT CARDS COST YOU MORE! And think about this...

If you have the money to pay off the credit card each month, WHY ARE YOU USING THE CARD IN THE FIRST PLACE?

Did you know, that when a retailer swipes your credit card, they are paying the credit card company 2 – 4 % of your purchase? That means, if you spend $100, the store is going to give as much as $4 to Visa, MasterCard, American Express, Discover or whomever. Now why would the retailer be willing to give money away?

Retailers want you to use credit cards because they want you to spend as much money as possible! If it costs a retailer a couple percentage points of the sale, it is worth it because the sale will be larger. How much larger? Or in other words, "How much more do people spend when they use a credit card?"

According to RAM Research...When people use credit cards, they spend as much as 212% of what they would spend with cash.

Most of us can relate to this. When you are shopping, and counting out money at the checkout, it's a little painful, isn't it? Cash is much more tangible – you feel it! Compare that to whipping out a credit card. When you throw the credit card down, it doesn't feel like "real" money does it?

We don't think of it as "three hundred dollars" or whatever you're spending. We think of it as "a few more bucks on my monthly payment…"

According to a Dunn & Bradstreet report "…the typical grocery purchase doubles when a credit card is used."[11] That means someone spends twice as much when they use a credit card instead of cash at the grocery store! Now, buying "too many" groceries isn't that bad since you probably will eat the food. But when you have a credit card, and aren't as worried about if you have enough money, do you think you might buy more gourmet foods, snack foods, prepared foods, deli foods, etc.? These items are of course among the more expensive and most profitable for the store.

Maybe you've noticed also that you can now buy much more than groceries at the grocery store. You can buy videos, flowers, books, etc. Again, these are higher-priced, higher margin items. Wouldn't you agree it is more likely that you will make impulse purchases like these when you are using a credit card?

Let's go back to that clothes shopping trip example. If you use cash, you spend $100. If you use a credit card, you might spend as much as $212. Is it worth it to the retailer to pay the 2 – 4% fee to the credit card company? Do the math!

Scenario 1 – Assume the retailer gets a 50% margin on the items you buy. That means for every dollar you spend, they keep 50 cents after paying the wholesale suppliers for the items you purchased. So, if you buy $100 worth of clothes with cash, the retailer gets to keep $50.

Scenario 2 – If you use your credit card, and spend $212 instead of the $100 you would have spent with cash, how much does the retailer end up with? If the store pays the highest credit card fees, they'll give about $8 to the credit card company. Again, assuming 50% margin, you buy $212 worth of clothes, the store has $106 left after paying the wholesalers. The retailer

11 Robert Klein, Dunn & Bradstreet Reports, March/April 1993

then pays an $8 credit card fee because you used a credit card. The store gets to keep $98 ($106 - $8 = $98).

So is it worth it to the store to pay a percentage of the sale amount to the credit card companies? Absolutely! Would you prefer to make $50 from a customer's purchases or would you rather pay $8 to the credit card companies and make $98 from the same customer's purchases!

Retailers have learned…

Credit Card Users Spend More Money!

It is obvious that they are trying to turn this fact into more profits. Have you noticed how stores have greatly increased their efforts to get you to use their cards? If they can get you to use their card, instead of Visa or some bankcard, then they keep all the fees and increase their profits! Often when you walk into a store, there is a table where some employee will encourage you to apply for their credit card and get "instant approval." Retailers are also using many different "bonuses" to encourage people to use their cards. For example:

- Many stores offer a 10 to 25% discount on your first purchase made with the credit card.
- Target donates 1% of purchase amounts made on their credit card to the school of your choice.
- Menards gives a 1% discount on all purchases on their card!

Don't get us wrong. We believe it is fine for businesses to make profits as long as they are ethical. And it is profits that drive the growth of credit cards. Retail stores are not in business for your convenience. They are in business to make a profit. They offer credit cards for one reason – credit cards increase sales and increased sales create more profit!

So when they make credit card offers, don't be "hypnotized" by the bonus they are offering folks, because…

2 - <u>There ain't no such thing as a free lunch.</u>

There are so many credit card bonuses out there. Cash back…donations to charity…frequent flier miles…frequent buyer points, etc. Ask yourself a question. Do you really think the credit card companies are just giving these things away? Are they just such nice people that they want to be as generous as possible?

There is a well-known fable that goes as follows…

Several thousand years ago, there was a young king. He ruled over a great land and had happy, loyal subjects. But he wanted more. He knew he needed great wisdom to make the kingdom an even better place to live. Being a king, as you might imagine, his ambitions were great, and he wanted to have all the wisdom in the world.

The king was educated and loved to read. He felt that much of the wisdom he did have came from books. If he could somehow gain the knowledge found in all the books in the world, he knew his wisdom would be great.

In those days however, books were rather rare and concentrated in seven libraries scattered across many lands. With his king duties, there was no way he could travel to all these lands and take the time to read all these books. Was there another way that he could gain the knowledge and increase his wisdom without traveling and reading all these books?

After thinking about his problem for some time, he summoned seven of his most talented scribes. He asked them to each travel to one of the seven libraries. Once they arrived at the library, they were to read each book and summarize all the knowledge they had in written form. The king felt if he could read a summary of all the world's books, he would then have great wisdom.

So the scribes set off on their journey. The king knew it would take some time, but he was surprised that it wasn't until seven years later, that all the scribes returned. Each had compiled a huge, thick volume of their notes. While the king was pleased to now be in possession of this knowledge, the kingdom was growing and required a great deal of his attention. There was no way he could read all seven of these large volumes because it would take months.

So he asked the scribes if they could summarize the seven volumes into something he could read much faster. The obedient scribes went to work. It took much effort to decrease the number of written pages while keeping the knowledge. Finally, after seven long years, they had completed their task and returned to the king.

The king was now a middle-aged man. While he was happy with the efforts of the scribes, when they presented him with one large volume containing all the wisdom of the world, he knew he still had a problem. It would take weeks to read the volume, and now that his kingdom was one of the largest in the world, he wouldn't have time to devote to reading.

Again he asked the scribes to condense the world's wisdom even further. In seven more years they came back with a seven-page summary. As the king was about to begin reading it, soldiers burst into the castle bringing news of an attack from a rival country. Though the king was now an old man, he jumped from his throne to lead his subjects into battle. As he was leaving, he gave the summary back to the scribes and asked them to condense it further.

Finally, after seven more long years, the scribes returned to the king. The king was now feeble and weak from age and war injuries. With great apologies, the scribes said they had at last gathered all the wisdom in the world and had summarized it as much as possible. The king was excited that after so many years, his quest for knowledge would be complete.

As the scribes unrolled the parchment and handed it to the king, his excitement grew too great for his tired and worn out heart. The king fell over dead as the parchment fell to the floor. There on the floor lay all the wisdom of the world, summarized in one sentence...

"There ain't no such thing as a free lunch!"

Okay, I can imagine all the moaning and groaning, but there is a purpose to this story relevant to credit cards. You may have noticed credit card companies offer such perks as "cash back bonuses" and "airline miles." While these perks sure seem tempting (who doesn't like free travel?), it's important to understand that especially with credit cards, "there ain't no such thing as a free lunch."

Promotions known as loyalty or frequent buyer programs were really started by the airlines. Remember when airlines started the frequent flyer programs in the early 80s? It was exciting because people liked the idea of earning free airline tickets as a reward for traveling with a specific airline.

Most airline customers are fickle – they fly on whatever airline has the best priced ticket. The frequent flyer programs were started because airlines were looking for a way to keep customers. The idea was to create loyalty. If a customer was focused on earning free tickets, and the way to earn tickets was to travel more, the airlines thought that perhaps they would not be as worried about price when choosing an airline for a trip.

Do you think the idea worked? It worked so well that corporations had to begin setting rules for their employees who traveled. Many of them would book a more expensive flight, in order to get frequent flyer miles on the airline they wanted, rather than save money with a different ticket.

Do you think the airlines lose money on the frequent flyer mileage? If they did, do you think they would continue to offer it? What airlines have found is that people are less concerned with cost when they feel they are getting something else for free!

This means that even though the airlines are giving away tickets, they come out ahead of the game financially. How can that be? Well, the free tickets have limitations and rules on their use. There is nothing wrong with that, but the end result is the free tickets end up being used to fill seats the airline would not have sold anyway. In other words, the free tickets don't reduce the airlines revenue. It also costs the same to fly the plane (give or take a couple of cans of Coke or Pepsi) regardless of the number of people onboard, so the free tickets don't increase the airline's cost.

The credit card industry saw the success of the airline rewards programs and decided to try the same thing. One of the best known and most popular credit card promotions is the Discover Card "Cash Back Bonus." This program has been so popular that now other cards are using it as well.

When you look at these promotions, you have to really look closely to see that "there is no free lunch." Let's look for example at the Cash Back Bonus rates for the Discover card and analyze the financial aspects.

According to the Discover website[12] you get up to 1% Cash Back on your purchases each year. The percentage is 0.25% on your first $1000 spent, 0.50% on your next $1000 spent, 0.75% on your third $1000 spent and 1% cash back bonus on spending on all purchases beyond the first $3000 you spend in a year. So the first thing to know about the Cash Back Bonus is that it is not a great deal of money.

The typical family has about an $8000 balance on their credit cards. If they had spent all of that money on a Discover card in one year, they would get a cash back bonus of about $65! That's $2.50 back on the first thousand, $5.00 back on the second thousand, $7.50 back on the third thousand and $10 per thousand for the next five thousand they spent. And by the way, though it is called a "cash-back" bonus, you don't get any cash. Your bonus is simply a credit that gets applied to your account!

Now $65 is nothing to sneeze at, but is it worth using your credit card often, and spending $8000 a year to get a $65 credit on your bill at the end of the year? Remember from our discussion above how people spend more money when they use credit cards than when they use cash. Let's look at the math.

If someone spends $8000 on their credit card, it is possible that they spent as much as 212% of what they would spend if they were using cash. This means they could spend as much as twice as much with a credit card as they would with cash. In other words if they had spent cash, they would have spent $4000. Instead, they used their credit card and spent $8000.

---

[12] http://www.discovercard.com/discover/data/apply/cashback.shtml

Now obviously, if someone spent $4000 more because they used a credit card, a $65 credit on their bill ("Cash Back Bonus") doesn't really mean much does it? Isn't spending $4000 more than you would have, really the same as WASTING $4000? Wouldn't you be much better off to not use the credit card and keep the $4000 instead of getting the $65 back?

Surely some of you are saying, "I don't believe everyone spends twice as much with a credit card as they would with cash." Fair enough. But can we agree that it is likely that most people will spend at least a little more when they use a credit card? How much is "a little more?"

…If they spend 50% more with a credit card, then the $65 cash back bonus cost them $2666 in extra spending.

…If they spend 10% more with a credit card, then the $65 cash back bonus cost them $727 in extra spending.

…If they spend JUST 1% more with a credit card, then the $65 cash back bonus cost them $79 in extra spending.

The only way you come out ahead with the Cash Back bonus award is if you DO NOT SPEND ONE PENNY MORE with the credit card than you do with cash. Someone would need to have a huge amount of discipline in order to not spend any more money with a credit card. Doesn't your personal experience tell you that you will spend at least a little more with a credit card than you will with cash?

Folks, if Discover lost money on the Cash Back Bonus, could they continue to offer the bonus and stay in business? Like the king learned many years ago…

There ain't no such thing as a free lunch!

The same idea applies to the idea of getting airline mileage from credit card spending. Cash back may get some people excited, but FREE TRAVEL really gets people's attention. But based on our discussion thus far, do you really think it is free? Let's look at the math on airline mileage from credit cards.

How much do you have to spend to get a free airline ticket? Typically, most credit cards will give you one mile for each dollar spent. A free domestic ticket (travel within the United States) usually requires 25,000 miles. Therefore, in order to get a free ticket by using your credit card, you will have to spend $25,000.

If someone spends $25,000 on their credit card in order to get a free ticket, do you think they spend any extra money that they would not have spent if they had used cash, or if they were not trying to get a "free" ticket?

How can something be "free" if you have to spend money to get it?

What is the value of an airline ticket? With all the options available for buying tickets and with a little effort, you can get a round trip ticket for around $300. But how much does that "free" ticket cost in terms of spending?

…If they spend 50% more with a credit card, then the $300 airline ticket cost them $8333 in extra spending.

…If they spend ONLY 10% more with a credit card, then the $300 airline ticket cost them $2273 in extra spending.

…If they spend JUST A MERE 1% more with a credit card, then the $300 airline ticket cost them $248 in extra spending.

We all love the idea of "free travel." As with the Cash Back Bonus award however, the only way you come out ahead with the airline mileage awards is if you DO NOT SPEND ONE PENNY MORE with the credit card than you do with cash. Do you really think that will happen?

Did you know the airlines don't just give the mileage to the credit companies? The credit card companies actually pay about 2 cents per mile you are awarded. Frequent flyer miles sold to airline partners are a source of revenue for the airlines. Now why would the credit card companies be spending this money on mileage? You already know the answer, don't you?

Credit card companies spend money on cash back, frequent flyer mileage and other promotions because they know additional credit card spending will more than pay for the promotions!

3 - <u>Minimum payments are designed to keep you in debt FOREVER!</u>

Minimum payments are a funny thing. Some people always make minimum payments. Some people pay off their credit cards each month. Most of us are somewhere in between these extremes. Has there ever been a time when you were short on money, and you were glad that you could just pay the minimum amount?

Minimum payments are convenient – they are easy. Typically, we analyze our financial situation based on how much money we have left over at the end of the month. Minimum payments trick us into thinking we have more money than we do.

Now we all know that minimum payments mean we pay more interest. But it's not that much interest, is it? In our classes we always ask people the following question…

"If you spend $2000 on your 17.9% credit card and make minimum payments, how long does it take you to pay off the debt?"

Most people say it will take five to 10 years to pay off this credit card with minimum payments. Hold onto your hats folks because the rest of the story is…

When making minimum payments, it takes 30 years and five months to pay off a 17.9% credit card with a $2000 balance!

If one chooses to pay this debt off with minimum payments, they will make a total of $6827 in payments, spending $4827 in interest! Now for those of you who are getting your slide rules or financial calculators out, there are a

114

number of unique factors inherent in credit card, or revolving credit, that make this different from a mortgage or car payment. The first factor to recognize with credit cards is that minimum payments are not necessarily level payments.

Have you ever noticed that your minimum payments on a credit card go up or down as your balance goes up or down? Minimum payments on credit cards are typically based on the current balance. They are calculated as a percentage of the balance. Minimum payments are generally 2% to 3% of the balance.

In this example, we used a minimum payment of 2%. With a $2000 debt, the minimum payment is therefore $40. If you make $40 payment every month, then the $2000 debt is paid off in seven years and nine months. But $40 is the minimum payment in the first month only!

After you have made the first minimum payment of $40, you no longer owe $2000. The $40 payment paid for $30 of interest and $10 of principal. So after the first payment, the balance is now $1990. Since minimum payment amount are calculated as a percentage of the balance, your minimum payment next month is 2% of $1990, or $39.80.

Are you beginning to see why minimum payments on credit cards can stretch your payments out for years and even decades? If you are on time with your payments, and you are slowly paying down your debt, what reward are you given? You are rewarded with reduced payments that allow you to continue paying on the debt for even longer!

If you think about the math, you will realize that you can never pay off a debt by only paying a percentage of the balance each month. At some point, you will have to pay more than 2% of the balance or the debt will continue forever! All credit cards have a minimum payment amount, usually in the range of $10 to $25. Eventually, if you are making minimum payments, your payment will be more than 2% of the balance. But it will still take you 30 to 40 years to pay off the balance.

For many people who make minimum payments, it can actually take even longer to pay off a debt. There are other factors that can increase the amount of time it takes to pay this $2000 credit card debt off. These factors include "take-a-month-off-promotion," late charges and penalties, and annual membership fees. When one is making minimum payments, there is NO ROOM FOR ERROR and these other factors come into play.

Have you ever received your credit card statement with a notice that says "Take a month off on us?" Sometimes, especially around the holidays, if you have kept current with your payments, you are given a month off from your payment. Do you think the credit card companies make this offer simply in the spirit of the season? Or do you think they are motivated by the additional interest they will earn? You can take a month off from payments, but the interest never takes even a day off! Your balance actually goes up and you didn't even buy anything!

How about late charges and penalties? Most people don't end up having these fees assessed, but would you agree that someone who is making minimum payments is more likely to have such a tight budget, that they miss a payment every once in a while?

Credit card companies make the most money from clients who make minimum payments. If someone makes minimum payments on their credit cards, they keep their debt longer and therefore pay more interest and other fees. All of this interest and these fees are money that you could be investing in your debt. Don't let the credit card companies take (though what they do is perfectly legal) what should be going towards the financial future of you and your loved ones.

Minimum payments are a "dual-edged" sword, meaning they can be good or bad for you. If in a month or two, your available cash is extra tight, minimum payments can be a blessing. But if you fall into the habit of making minimum payments, like any habit, it can be difficult to change.

Minimum payments are a slippery slope. Just like using credit cards in general, the more often you use minimum payments, the easier it is to do. Minimum payments can become a treadmill that you never are able to get off. The minimum payment trap is a vicious cycle, which once you get in deep enough can be almost impossible to break.

The IYD Inc. specialists can offer people who have fallen into this vicious cycle information on different programs that can help them out of their situation. IYD recommendations have helped thousands of clients begin their escape from the cycle of minimum debt payments. These clients are good people who have experienced some bad times. Some of them earn less than $15,000 a year. Some earn more than $100,000 a year. It can happen to anyone regardless of his or her financial circumstances. The point is this…

Regardless of your income, you must avoid minimum payments at all costs, or you stand the chance of losing your financial future!

Get started today with your own *Invest in Your Debt* program! Break the bonds of minimum payments. After following the IYD program for a short time, you will be free of minimum payments forever. Once you break free of minimum payments, you will be able to invest in your debt at a maximum level. And once you invest in your debt, you will be able to achieve true financial freedom.

We've said it before, but again you see, it is a choice. You can ignore all of this information, continue making minimum payments and face a lifetime of financial bondage. Or you can invest in your debt, by first breaking the minimum payment cycle and look forward to a lifetime of true financial freedom.

4 - <u>Credit card companies that offer you a card when no one else will are not your friend!</u>

This last secret goes against what you would intuitively think. Imagine this scenario if you have not already experienced it. Money is tight in your family, perhaps your credit cards are charged to their limit and you are worried about the "what if" scenarios. You know, "what if I need new tires for the car," "what if the kids get a bunch of cavities," etc. Maybe you send in a few of the credit card applications you get in the mail, "just in case you need them" and find out that you are rejected for the new credit cards. You have reached your credit limit or maybe have some bad credit history.

Then one day you get another credit card application and you send it in, hoping you will "get lucky." A couple of weeks later, a brand new credit card arrives in the mail, ready to solve your financial problems. You feel like the luckiest person around because now you've got a financial safety net again. Our initial thoughts might be "boy, what a great credit card company – they gave me a chance when no one else would." Little do you realize that you are the one doing the credit card company the favor.

The fastest growing segment of the credit card industry is what is known as the "sub-prime" segment. Sub-prime refers to people who would not qualify for new or additional credit under typical credit guidelines. The reasons people would not qualify vary, but they might include bad credit histories, a high debt to income ratio or low income. Why are people who are generally not "credit-worthy" the fastest growing segment of the credit card industry?

Many credit card companies make the bulk of their profits from sub-prime clients!

A number of credit card companies specialize in sub-prime clients. You might be familiar with some of these companies such as MBNA, Providian, First USA and more. We would assume that clients who are in tight financial situations don't have much disposable income. So how can a credit card company make money on clients who don't have much money?

Credit card companies make piles of money from sub-prime clients, because those clients have no choice but to pay high costs!

Now when you sign up for one of these sub-prime cards, it appears to be like most any other card, and it really is to a large degree, as long as you follow their rules. You usually have a low introductory rate and no annual fee. But remember, in our example above, very few companies would give you a card because you are a credit risk. The companies that issue sub-prime cards may actually be hoping you break their rules!

What rules are we talking about? Simple rules like paying your bill on time, not exceeding your credit limit, etc. These are typical rules for most cards. But when you break them, by law, credit companies have the right to impose "punitive" interest and fees. Do you know what punitive interest and fees mean?

Punitive literally means "punishment." So when a credit card company charges you punitive interest and fees they are punishing you for not following the rules!

Now you may have gotten a card with a low introductory interest rate. Usually after a few months, you know that rate will go up to some constant rate. If however, you are even one day late with a payment, the credit card company can raise your rate to a punitive level! According to Cardweb, punitive interest rates on credit cards are now as high as 31.9%![13]

But that's not all. Late fees can be added to your account balance. Sometimes these fees can end up being hundreds of dollars. How can that happen?

If you are already in the position of only being able to make minimum payments, and now you have late fees added on, your late fees can be added to your minimum payment. If you are already having trouble making the minimum payment, and now it is increased with late fees, are you going to have any easier time making the now larger payment? Of course not. So next month you will still be considered late because you haven't made the minimum payment. What happens then? More late fees!

But it gets even worse folks. What if you are nearing your credit limit on a sub-prime card? If you go over the limit, you can then be charged additional punitive interest charges and fees. Many cards will let you go over the limit – it just gives them the opportunity to collect more fees! Since late charges are added to your balance, they too could push you over your limit if you are close!

---

[13] www.cardweb.com

It doesn't take more than a late payment or two or going over your limit just once to lock you into years of sky-high interest and fees. So if you get fed up with all these high costs, can't you just transfer the balance to a different credit card company and be done with it? Usually not. Remember the reason you got this sub-prime card is that you couldn't get a card from anyone else. Now that you are in trouble with your sub-prime card, your credit rating is even worse. Why would another credit card company want your business now?

Sub-prime cards are "fool's gold," folks. It seems great that you are able to get a card when no one else will give you one. But that is precisely the reason you should avoid such cards like the plague. It is a great "catch-22." The sub-prime cards want you because no one else will take you. Because of this, they know you are more than likely to be late on a payment or exceed your credit limit. And when you do, such companies are hovering like vultures, waiting to make money from your financial misfortune!

SUMMARY

Like any good business, the goal of credit card companies is to make a profit and maximize value for their shareholders. Yes, businesses should serve their customers, but unless they make a profit, they won't be able to stay in business. If they go out of business, they won't be able to serve many customers, will they?

So don't get angry at the credit card companies because they are trying to be good businesses. Just understand how their businesses operate and how they make their money. That way, you can make sure that you minimize your costs, and your money goes towards building your wealth instead of building the credit card company's profits. Hopefully, these four secrets give you some insight you did not have before.

The best approach to credit cards is to change your financial life so you never need them again. If you follow the linear math / variable path process we teach for investing in your debt, you can quickly reach a point where you never use a credit card again. Your instructor and everyone associated with

IYD Inc. (IYD) is dedicated to helping you reach this point in your life, where compound interest is working for you, and not against you.

Chapter 7

Pay off your Mortgage? What? Are you stupid?

Answer a quick question – **"Do you own your own home?"**

When we ask people in our classes "who owns their own home," most people instinctively raise their hands. Did you answer "yes?" Investing in your Debt is about choices and one of the important choices is how we choose to look at things. The way we look at things, our perspective, greatly influences our motivation to change things. When it comes to mortgages folks, we need to get a fresh perspective of reality.

According to US Census Bureau data, most people have a mortgage.[14] John Cumutta, author of the well-known book *Debt Free and Prosperous Living*, says that when you look across our population, and include everybody, the truth is…

Less than 2% of Americans "home owners" actually own their own home![15]

More people owned their homes in the 30's, 40's, 50's, 60's, 70's, 80's and even the 90's than do today. Doesn't that seem strange when you consider we have had the greatest of economic booms over the last ten to twenty years? We have experienced the greatest economy ever, yet only 2% of people own their homes.

Think about the "Do you own your own home?" question again. Do you **really** own your home? Or does the mortgage company own your home? Students tell us that if they have a homeowners insurance claim, when they get the insurance check, they are quickly reminded who owns their home. The check is made out to the mortgage company!

---

[14] http://www.census.gov/hhes/www/housing/ahs/ahs97/tab315.html

15 John Cummuta, *Debt-FREE & Prosperous Living*, 8th ed. (Boscobel, WI:Debt-FREE & Prosperous Living, Inc., 1998)

In reality, most of us are paying rent for our homes. The rent is either paid to a landlord or to a mortgage company. We don't really own the home, until the last payment is made, do we? Think I'm wrong? Try missing a payment or two and you'll find out quickly who owns your home!

We make this point for a couple of reasons. We want to help people "deal with the reality" of home ownership. This can be a challenge because most people have a significant emotional attachment to their homes. In fact people often overvalue their house in their minds.

If you ask them how many bedrooms they have, they count an extra bedroom they plan on building someday. When describing the square footage, they include the space in the unfinished basement! If you were to ask them what their house is worth, the value is usually overstated by 20% or more. Now there's certainly nothing wrong with being proud of your house. But this pride can blind us from the financial reality of home ownership. Think about this...

Are you so proud of your house that you would pay for it three times?

Let's say you find a house you would like to buy, and the price is $150,000. Would you tell the owner "Your price is much too low – I insist on paying $350,000!" Of course you wouldn't. But the financial reality of mortgages is just that. When you pay a mortgage over 30 years, you will pay for the house several times over.

You've probably realized by this point that our idea of debt elimination includes paying off your mortgage. The idea of paying off your mortgage however, for most people, is totally contrary to our conventional way of thinking. The idea of having a mortgage is so ingrained in our thinking as something that is just a given. It is a certainty in life, like death and taxes. All people have mortgages, don't they? No. They don't. Just ask the millionaires in *The Millionaire Next Door*!

As you read this book...when you attend one of our workshops around the country...you will discover the secret to true financial freedom. That secret is of course that most people can best create wealth by first eliminating their debt. But there is one critical component to this approach. There is one thing YOU MUST DO, or in all likelihood you will not achieve financial freedom.

To achieve true financial freedom, you must first eliminate your debt and most importantly, you must ELIMINATE YOUR MORTGAGE!

People with real wealth (not those with wealth "on paper") don't have mortgages. They don't pay compound interest – they only earn compound interest! Most of us have never heard this secret from Wall Street experts, from financial planners or especially from our mortgage officers. In fact, we've probably read, learned or been given advice that is exactly the opposite. Most of us think of our mortgages as something other than debt.

It's funny when we talk to people about eliminating debt. Most folks think our mission of eliminating all debt on this planet is terrific, but they think our mission is directed at someone else. They say, "The work you do is terrific" but they also say "I don't have any debt..." When we ask them if they have a mortgage they say "Well...yeah, but I don't have any debt!"

So it is important that we try to help people change their thinking about mortgages. If you see mortgages as some type of unimportant factor in your financial life, you probably will not be motivated to free yourself from their wealth-draining process. As Robert Kiyosaki points out in *Rich Dad, Poor Dad,* a house is a liability, not an asset. We would modify that slightly and agree that it is a liability, but only while you are making payments. Your home can become an asset once it is paid for.

As Kiyosaki states, "A liability takes money out of your pocket each month. An asset puts money in your pocket."[16] While you are making debt payments on your mortgage, money is leaving your pocket – that is the definition of a liability. Once you have paid off your mortgage, you no longer have to make a mortgage payment (or rent payment!). That money you save on housing costs is put back into your pocket. That is the definition

---

16 Robert Kiyosaki, *Rich Dad, Poor Dad* (New York, NY: Warner Books, Inc., 2000)

of an asset! If you recognize mortgages as the huge barrier to true financial freedom that they are for most people, then you'll be more likely to make some positive changes.

We devote a whole chapter to mortgages because we want you to achieve true financial freedom. The quickest and most reliable method for achieving this is to first invest in your debt and eliminate it, then use the money you had been wasting on debt payments to begin building wealth. If you don't pay off your mortgage, you cannot eliminate your debt. If you don't eliminate your debt…well, then your chances of achieving true financial freedom are quite small.

Now remember, one of the unique aspects of the *Invest in Your Debt* program is that the plan is practical. Our plan needs to be able to weather the financial storms that hit our lives. If the IYD program can't help you handle the challenges that come up as you make your journey to debt freedom, then it really isn't of great value. The plan must deal with the realities of the "real world."

One of the "Real World" issues you will face after reading this book or attending one of our classes is people will think you are **crazy!** If you were to tell your best friend, or maybe even your spouse that you plan on investing in your debt, including paying off your mortgage early, way ahead of schedule, how do you think they'd react? They'd probably say…

Pay off your Mortgage? What? Are you stupid?

Don't be discouraged by this reaction. Remember, what we teach is contrary to "Conventional Wisdom." According to John Cummuta, 96% of people fail because they follow conventional wisdom.[17] This is based on US Department of Health and Human Services studies showing that only 4% of people are financially independent at age 65. For most of us, however, our financial knowledge consists primarily of this conventional wisdom. The

---

17 John Cummuta, *Debt-FREE & Prosperous Living*, 8th ed. (Boscobel, WI:Debt-FREE & Prosperous Living, Inc., 1998)

IYD plan for true financial freedom goes against the grain of what most of us have previously learned.

When people laugh at your idea of investing in your debt, understand that it is a normal reaction. You too probably thought the idea of first investing in your debt, and then eliminating it, was far-fetched, maybe even impossible, until you learned how easy, practical and smart it really is. You now have the opportunity to make this world a better place and educate others on the benefits of investing in your debt. More importantly, you need to first educate yourself on why this approach, and especially, eliminating your mortgage makes such good financial sense.

Now once your friends pick themselves up off the floor after their hysterical laughing fit, they will probably feel they need to set you straight. With the best of intentions, they'd probably remind you of the reasons why a mortgage is "good." You know…

1) Your interest rate is only 8% (or whatever your interest rate is) – that's cheap money
2) It's the last tax break you'll ever have
3) Why pay extra on your mortgage when you can do much better by investing the money in the stock market

We call these "reasons" the three great myths of mortgages. We want to debunk **these myths** because they **promote ideas that prevent most people from achieving true financial freedom.**

Believe it or not, mortgages are a big part of most people's financial failure. It's not that we are against mortgages or that mortgages are inherently a bad thing. It's just that the way most people use mortgages condemns them to a life of financial struggle.

Let's take a look at the lack of logic in these myths…

MYTH #1 – Your Interest Rate is Low

Often in our classes, we will ask people "who has a good interest rate on their mortgage?" Usually, most of the students in the class raise their hand. Most people believe they have a good interest rate. That's natural, isn't it? If someone thinks they don't have a good interest rate, aren't they going to do something about it? Especially during the refinancing frenzy of the last few years, more people than ever have a "good" or low interest rate.

The problem with Myth #1 is that it distracts you from the most important issue. Here's the "Rest of the Story" concerning low interest rates on mortgages…

Most people don't have a 6%, 7% or 8% mortgage…most people have a 67% mortgage!

I bet your mortgage broker or banker has never told you that! We'll prove that most people have a 67% mortgage later in this chapter. But for now, we need to highlight a point.

We shouldn't be worrying about interest rates so much because the real "hidden time bomb" in our mortgage is the **total cost of interest**. Interest rates affect our payments, but the total cost of interest affects our financial future. Focusing on interest rates is potentially very dangerous because it lulls us into a false sense of security. If we feel comfortable that we have a low interest then we don't bother noticing how **huge the total amount of money we pay in interest really is!**

We have to get away from conventional wisdom when it comes to mortgage rates. We have been misled regarding the real cost of mortgages. When people get caught up thinking about good or low interest rates, their attention is diverted from the real issue. Do you remember when you closed your last mortgage? All the documents to be signed can be pretty confusing. But there is one very important form called the Federal Truth-in-Lending Disclosure Statement.

When you looked at your Truth-in-Lending form, you saw the interest rate and the amount of the loan. This form also lists two other critical numbers…the cost of credit (total dollars of interest to be paid) and the total payments. We promise you, anyone who has ever seen these numbers has felt their heart skip a beat when they signed the mortgage documents.

Along with the Truth-in-Lending forms, the mortgage companies are at least practicing truth in advertising. Do you know what the word mortgage comes from the Latin language? Mortgage is the combination of two Latin words, mortus, meaning "death," and gage, meaning "grip." So literally, your mortgage is a "death grip!" We're not joking here! In the Roman times of Caesar, if you had a debt, you pledged your life against it. If you did not repay your debt you paid for it with your life. If we had those types of debt laws today there would probably be many fewer bankruptcies. (That's a joke folks – it's okay to laugh).

The Truth-in-Lending documents show the REAL COST OF INTEREST. Guess what?

In most cases the amount of money paid for interest on a mortgage by far exceeds the price of the house!

The human mind is designed to protect us. A primary instinct is self-preservation. If we are confronted by an overwhelming, frightening experience, our mind often blocks the memory. You would be surprised, if you talk to someone who just closed on a mortgage. Many people don't remember the cost of credit or the total payment numbers. This is just their mind protecting them. Why? Because the numbers are so outrageous!

In order to get the proper mindset regarding mortgages, you need to realize that from the perspective of true financial freedom, interest rates are not the most important issue. They don't reflect the impact that a mortgage has on your financial life. We bring this point up because when mortgages are advertised, all of the attention is usually focused on the interest rate. Though we may assume otherwise, interest rate alone really tells you little about the cost of interest.

When it comes to mortgages, the total cost of the interest to be paid is much more important than the interest rate.

We think if we have an interest rate of 6%, 7% or 8%, then we have a good rate. Most people tend to equate interest rate with the amount of interest they pay. We think rate is the same as cost. You know, "I have an 8% interest rate so I pay 8% interest." But interest rate is very different from interest cost.

For example, let's say you bought a $150,000 house with a 30-year, 8% mortgage. Is your interest cost 8% of the purchase price, or in other words, $12,000 (8% of $150,000)?

Your interest cost is only equal to the interest rate if you pay off the mortgage in the first year!

The interest cost is actually 8% per year, for many, many years. Many of us have heard that total payments on a mortgage are much more than the cost of the house. But have you ever stopped to figure out how much you really pay in interest? Most of us don't bother to figure out the total cost of interest because somewhere in the back of our minds we know that cost is frightening. The general rule of thumb relating total payments to purchase price is as follows:

On a typical 30-year mortgage, paid over 30 years, your total payments will be two to three times more than the price of the house.

In other words, when you add up all your payments, your $150,000 house cost you $300,000 to $450,000. Now does that sound like an 8% mortgage? Let's look at the total payments for a $150,000 on a 30-year mortgage at different interest rates.

Interest Rate	6.0%	7.0%	8.0%	9.0%	10.0%
Total Payments	$323,968	$359,223	$395,883	$434,399	$474,573
Cost of House	$150,000	$150,000	$150,000	$150,000	$150,000

Looking at this table, you can easily see how the actual amount you pay over 30 years on your mortgage is really several times more than the cost of the house. When you think about it, doesn't it seem crazy? For example, if you have an 8% mortgage, you actually pay $395,883 for your $150,000 house.

Let's look at it from a perspective that will really make things seem out of whack. How much interest do you think is paid on these mortgages? Remember, the purchase price is $150,000 so the total interest paid would be calculated by subtracting the principal amount ($150,000) from the total payments.

Interest Rate	6.0%	7.0%	8.0%	9.0%	10.0%
Total Payments	$323,968	$359,223	$395,883	$434,399	$474,573
Cost of House	$150,000	$150,000	$150,000	$150,000	$150,000
Cost of Interest	$173,968	$209,223	$245,883	$284,399	$324,573

While interest rates themselves seem like small numbers, you can see how the total cost of interest is in reality extremely high! If you have a 9.0% mortgage, you will pay $284,399 just in interest over 30 years.

You will pay about TWICE AS MUCH IN INTEREST as you actually pay for the house!

Look at these numbers and become aware of the psychological effect they can have on people. If your mortgage broker, who has just approved your

$150,000 mortgage, said "We have approved your mortgage and it will only cost you $284,399 in interest payments." Do you think that mortgage broker is going to have many clients? Instead, your mortgage broker speaks in "conventional wisdom-speak" and says, "Your mortgage is at 9%." That sounds much better, doesn't it?

Now ask yourself a question. What aspect of your mortgage impacts your financial life more directly? Whether you have a 7% or 8% interest rate, or whether you pay $200,000 to $300,000 in interest? Which more accurately represents the cost of your mortgage?

Saying "I have a 7% mortgage" doesn't represent the total cost of interest. It is simply the interest rate. If we really want to be honest and "real" about interest and rates, another number to look at is interest payment rate. Interest payment rate is the percentage of each payment that is interest.

Have you looked at your mortgage payment coupon lately? Usually they show how much of your payment goes towards principal (a small amount for most people) and how much goes to interest (a big amount). For example, if you make a $1000 monthly mortgage payment, how much of that payment goes towards principal and how much goes to interest? If you have been paying on your 8%, 30-year mortgage for five years, approximately…

$910 of your $1000 payment goes to interest and only $90 goes to principal!

What on average is the percentage of each payment that goes towards interest? In other words, for each dollar you send into your mortgage company, how much does the mortgage company keep for interest and how much goes to reduce your debt?

We calculate interest payment rate simply by dividing the total interest payments by total payments. Look at the following table:

Interest Rate	6.0%	7.0%	8.0%	9.0%	10.0%
Total Payments	$323,968	$359,223	$395,883	$434,399	$474,573
Cost of House	$150,000	$150,000	$150,000	$150,000	$150,000
Cost of Interest	$173,968	$209,223	$245,883	$284,399	$324,573
Interest Payment Rate	53.7%	58.2%	62.1%	65.5%	68.4%

What do these numbers mean? Well, if you are the typical family with a mortgage interest rate of about 7%, you have an interest payment rate of 58.2%. This means…

Out of every dollar you send to your mortgage company, 58.2% goes towards interest.

In our classes, for the purpose of easy math we use the example of a typical $100,000 house. If you have a 9.5% mortgage rate on a 30-year loan, you will make a total of $300,000 in payments. That means you pay $200,000 in interest payments. Therefore, if $200,000 out of $300,000 in payments goes towards interest, or 67% of each dollar, isn't it proper to say…

YOU HAVE A 67% MORTGAGE!

Hopefully now you understand the thought process behind this statement. While it is true that your interest rate may be 7% or 8%, it is also true that 67 cents from every dollar you pay to the mortgage company goes to interest. Based on this reality, which number best represents how your mortgage impacts your financial future? Is it an 8% mortgage or a 67% mortgage?

Do you see why the typical fascination with interest rates is so non-productive? It isn't interest rates that erode our wealth. It is the total cost of interest and the percentage of every dollar we pay to the mortgage company that goes to interest.

If you compare a 7% rate to a 9% rate, it seems that the 7% is much better, doesn't it? But when you consider that even with a 7% interest rate, you will still pay over $200,000 in interest, the interest rate doesn't seem as significant any more.

This is where we want to encourage your thinking to be. Recognize that it is the total cost of interest that is most important, not the interest rate. Don't let the "low-rate sirens" cause your financial ship to crash on the rocks of total interest cost. Once we focus on the important percentage, we can be better motivated to invest in our debt and therefore eliminate the cost of interest.

Now we say our typical family has an interest payment rate of 58.2%, but this is a little misleading because it is an average over 30 years. On a 30-year mortgage, interest is front-loaded. What we mean is that in the early years of the mortgage, much more interest is paid than in later years.

Take a look at the following table to see what percentage of your mortgage payment goes to interest, depending on your interest rate and how many years you've paid on your 30-year mortgage…

What Percentage of each Mortgage Payment is Interest?

Number of Years Left on Mortgage						
	30 years	25 years	20 years	15 years	10 years	5 years
Interest Rate						
6%	83 %	78 %	70 %	59 %	45 %	26 %
7%	88 %	83 %	75 %	65 %	50 %	29 %
8%	91 %	86 %	80 %	70 %	55 %	33 %
9%	93 %	89 %	83 %	74 %	59 %	36 %
10%	95 %	92 %	86 %	78 %	63 %	39 %

Our typical family, the Spendsmart family, has a 7.11% mortgage interest rate. We know over the life of their mortgage, of each dollar they send to their mortgage company, 52.8% on average goes to pay interest. As you can see from the above table however, in the first five years of the mortgage they spend 88% of each mortgage payment dollar on interest. As they get in the last few years of the mortgage, less than 30% of each mortgage payment dollar goes to mortgage interest.

The front-loaded nature of mortgages, where you pay much more of the interest in the early years as opposed to the later years of the mortgage, is one of the "dirty little secrets" of the "death grip" (remember, death grip is what the word mortgage means in Latin). Though it's not illegal…

The front-loading of interest in mortgages is a silent thief that steals people's wealth without them even knowing it!

The typical family pays an average of 52.8% mortgage interest cost, **only if they stay in the same house for 30 years!**

How long have you lived in your house? How long did you live in the previous house? The nature of our society has become one where we move frequently. Jobs changes, family changes and many other factors have made us a very mobile society. How often do we move? According to the National Association of Realtors, we move on average every seven years.

If we move every seven years, how does this impact the cost of interest? Look at the chart above. In the first seven years of a mortgage, you will be in the range of 80% or 90% interest payments. In other words, of each dollar you send to the mortgage company, 80% to 90% goes to interest payments.

Now we know this percentage goes down over time…

But most people stay in the 80 – 90 % interest range on their mortgage forever!

How can this be true? Think about it – if we move every seven years, does our mortgage move with us? Of course not! So we get a new mortgage when we move. Now, since we had been paying on the old mortgage for seven years, do we get a new 23-year mortgage? NO – we start over again with a new 30-year mortgage.

So the typical family who moves every seven years continues to make mortgage payments that are in the early years of the mortgage! They continue to make payments that are in the 80 – 90 % interest range! They never get to the later years of a mortgage where a greater amount of each dollar they send goes to principal and less goes to interest. The same logic applies to re-financing an existing mortgage. Even if you don't move, when you refinance, you start over with a new 30-year mortgage and 90%+ interest payments!

Now, of course, we are not against moving. We just want to demonstrate how a traditional aspect of our society makes the cost of mortgage interest even higher! There is nothing wrong with moving. Just use the IYD system and OWN YOUR HOUSE FREE AND CLEAR before you move the next time. Then you will actually be in a position to pay cash for your next home!

So folks, if you really want to have the proper perspective about mortgage interest rates, here's the truth…

While most people are focused on whether their mortgage interest RATE is 7 or 8%, they are blind to the fact that their total mortgage interest COST is 80 or 90%!

Now that you understand the "rest of the story" concerning mortgage interest rates, we hope it helps motivate you to eliminate this expense from your life by first investing in your debt and then eliminating every debt, including your mortgage. The next time someone tells you your mortgage interest rate is "cheap money" tell them you don't think 80% interest cost is cheap!

Let's move on to the next mortgage myth…

MYTH # 2 – Mortgage Interest is the last Tax Break you'll ever have!

When we talk about paying off the mortgage in class, our seminar leaders know someone is going to raise their hand. They'll have a little smile on their face because they think they've got us, they think they've found the flaw in what we teach about investing in your debt. They ask us…

"What about the mortgage interest tax deduction?"

We know most people are thinking about this question to themselves, so we always appreciate someone asking in class. We talked earlier about how people are emotionally attached to their houses. People are even more attached to their tax deductions!

The mortgage interest tax deduction is one of the few remaining deductions most people have. The number of tax deductions we have seems to have shrunk tremendously. We are certainly not against tax deductions. Our position on the mortgage interest tax deduction is this…

Take the mortgage interest tax deduction as long as you have a mortgage, but the deduction is not a good reason to hang on to your mortgage!

Again, you can choose to look at this issue from a number of perspectives. Let's look at it from a very simple perspective. Assume you are in the 28 % tax bracket. Consider this question…

"Will you give someone $1, if they give you 28 cents in return?"

Would anyone like to take that offer? We can give out piles of 28 pennies and would love to trade them for dollars all day long!

OF COURSE YOU WOULDN'T TAKE THAT DEAL. But think about it folks, that's the deal we take with the mortgage interest tax deduction. For every dollar we spend in mortgage interest, we get 28 cents back on our taxes. Does it make any sense to keep paying a dollar and getting 28 cents back if there is a better alternative? We do get crazy about our tax deductions. We hire accountants and tax attorneys to do our taxes so we can pay as little as possible. And it is true that we pay less in taxes if we have a mortgage. But when it costs us $1 in interest costs to save 28 cents on taxes, wouldn't you just rather keep the dollar? Wouldn't you rather pay 28 cents more in taxes, but keep the $1 in interest and be 72 cents ahead?

Here's the math:

With Mortgage Interest Deduction

> You spend $1 on interest – you save 28 cents on your taxes – your net cost is 72 cents.

Without Mortgage Interest Deduction

> You spend $0 on interest – you spend 28 cents (more) on taxes – your net cost is 28 cents.

The mortgage interest tax deduction is a great example of how conventional wisdom can get out of hand, especially when people don't really think things through and blindly follow such advice. Even worse, often in classes, we will hear stories about people whose tax advisors have told them to buy a bigger house **just so they can get a bigger tax deduction!** From solely a tax perspective it might be the right answer, but from a real wealth-building point of view it is devastating advice!

Folks, if you have a tax advisor who has ever told you to buy a bigger house so you can have a bigger deduction, you need to run, not walk, and find a new advisor immediately. Think about what that advice boils down to – they are telling you to spend a bunch of additional money on interest so you can get a little bit more back on your taxes. Now how does that make sense?

But there is an even more important aspect of the mortgage interest tax deduction. We have been assuming that you gain 28 cents for each dollar spent on interest when using the deduction. While it's true that you may get 28 cents back, **you don't get 28 "extra" cents back!**

What we mean by this is to qualify for the mortgage interest tax deduction, you give up some other deductions. So while you are getting a decrease in taxes with your mortgage interest deduction, you are also increasing your taxes by giving up other deductions. This means your tax benefit is something less than 28 cents.

To truly analyze the benefit of the mortgage interest tax deduction you have to look at the **marginal tax benefit**. Now don't let these accounting words scare you. What we mean by this is **"how much additional tax benefit do you get from the mortgage interest tax deduction?"**

For example, even if you do not have a mortgage, you will get to use what are known as "Standard Deductions." The magnitude of these deductions varies according to a number of factors including such things as the number of dependents you have and marital status.

If you want to take the mortgage interest tax deduction, you must "itemize" your taxes. When you itemize your taxes, you are no longer eligible to use the standard deductions. Therefore, to truly analyze the benefit of the mortgage interest tax deduction, you need to compare how much you would pay in taxes if you had no mortgage interest (so then you would take the standard deduction) versus how much you pay in taxes when you do have mortgage interest (when you itemize your taxes).

You know you will save some on taxes because of the standard deduction. The question is, **"How much additional money will I save on taxes if I have mortgage interest to deduct?"** This is what we mean by "marginal tax benefit" – how much more you will save on taxes.

Let's look at how things work out for our typical family. They currently make $51,181 in annual income. Let's see how they do with their mortgage income tax deduction.

First we subtract the standard deduction and personal exemptions from our typical family's income. Since they will be itemizing their deductions, they will not be able to use the standard deduction. According to IRS publication 501, the personal exemption was $2750 for each person whom the Spendsmart family can claim as a dependent.[18] This includes themselves and their two children. This means the Spendsmart family gets to deduct $11,000 (4 times $2750) from their income before calculating their taxes.

Since the Spendsmarts will be itemizing their deductions and taking the mortgage interest tax deduction, we need to look at how much interest they paid on their mortgage. People often confuse this point…

You do not get to deduct YOUR ENTIRE MORTGAGE PAYMENT…you can only deduct THE AMOUNT YOU PAID IN INTEREST!

So while our typical family pays $9084 on their mortgage, they only get to deduct the interest payments. Since they are early in their mortgage, the amount of interest they are paying is high. During the last 12 months (months 12 – 23 of their mortgage), based on amortization schedules, they made $1344.69 in principal payments and $7739.31 in interest payments on their first mortgage.

Now remember they have a home equity loan as well. There are a variety of regulations regarding the deductibility of interest on home equity loans. For example, you cannot deduct all interest on the portion of a loan that exceeds the equity the homeowner has. For the purpose of this example, however, we will assume our typical family is able to deduct all of the interest they paid on their home equity loan as well. In the last 12 months (months 21 – 32 on the amortization schedule), they made $1723.50 in principal payments and $2944.50 in interest payments on their second mortgage (home equity loan).

So over the last twelve months, the Spendsmart family has made a total of $13,752 in mortgage and home equity loan payments. Of these payments,

---

[18] http://www.irs.gov/prod/forms_pubs/pubs/p50104.htm

only $3068.19 has gone to principal! This means $10,683.81 of the payments has gone towards interest.

All these interest payments are good news in terms of taxes. Think again however, how much better off would our typical family be if they didn't have any debt. The Spendsmarts would have kept all of those interest payments, over $10,000 this year alone, for other things more important to them. Unless the tax savings are more than the $10,000 they paid in interest, there is no way they can come out ahead. However, since they still have the debt, let's figure out the tax picture:

Gross Income: $51,181
Personal Exemption: ($11,000)
Mortgage Interest Deduction: ($10,684)

Adjusted Gross Income: $29,497

According to IRS tax tables on their website,[19] the Spendsmarts would pay $4421 in taxes. This includes all the personal exemptions and the mortgage interest tax deduction.

Now let's see how much financial sense it makes for them to get debt free. If they choose to first invest in their debt, then eliminate their debt and follow the IYD plan to true financial freedom, how would this impact their taxes?

To answer this question we need to determine what their taxes would be without the mortgage interest tax deduction. Since they will not be itemizing (they won't have a mortgage interest tax deduction), our typical family will be eligible for the standard deduction, which according to the IRS website[20] would be $7200 for married-filing-jointly taxpayers.

---

[19] http://www.irs.gov/prod/ind_info/tax_tables/tbl_030k.html
[20] http://www.irs.gov/prod/tax_edu/teletax/tc551.html

Their tax situation would look like this:

Gross Income:	$51,181
Personal Exemption:	($11,000)
Standard Deduction:	($7,200)
Adjusted Gross Income:	$32,981

According to IRS tax tables on their web site,[21] our typical family would pay $4946 in taxes. This includes all the personal exemptions and the mortgage interest tax deduction.

So, did having the mortgage tax deduction make a big difference in this family's financial life? Let's do a side-by-side comparison:

	With Mortgage Interest Tax Deduction	Without Mortgage Interest Tax Deduction
Income	$51,181	$51,181
Personal Exemption	-$11,000	-$11,000
Mortgage Interest Deduction	-$10,684	$0
Standard Deduction	$0	-$7200
Adjusted Gross Income	$29,497	$32,981
Federal Income Tax Due	$4,421	$4,946
Tax Savings/Cost	$525	-$525

$525!!!!!!

For our typical family that wonderful mortgage tax deduction saves them $525 in taxes! If this is the biggest tax deduction you have left, then it

---

[21] http://www.irs.gov/prod/ind_info/tax_tables/tbl_035k.html

doesn't seem like it's worth getting excited about. Five hundred twenty-five dollars in tax savings is the reason some tax advisors tell their clients to buy a larger house. This $525 in tax savings is the justification for millions of home equity loans. The bottom line is this folks…

Our typical family spends $10,684 in interest in order to save $525 on their taxes!

Now does that really make any sense? Follow the IYD plan and pay your mortgage off early. During the time you still have your mortgage, of course you should take the deduction. But pay your mortgage off as quickly as possible because…

You are much better off saving thousands of dollars on interest than saving a few hundred dollars on taxes.

There is another important fact in the "Rest of the Story" about the mortgage interest tax deduction. Most people assume you get the deduction for as long as you have a mortgage. This is not the case. Remember, to get the deduction, you must be able to itemize your deductions. You need a certain level of deductions to be able to itemize.

We already know that over time, the amount of interest you pay on your mortgage goes down. Eventually, the mortgage interest you pay will not be enough to allow you to qualify for itemizing. So unless you have many other deductible expenses, such as high medical bills, high state taxes or business expenses, you will not be able to deduct your mortgage interest deduction forever.

But even if you could always deduct your mortgage interest, is that a reason to keep your financial death grip? Is the mortgage interest deduction a reason to continue to pay thousands of dollars in interest each year? Of course not!

Please note, this information should not be taken as tax advice. But let's look at mortgage interest from a common sense perspective. Here is the choice the Spendsmart family faces. They can follow the IYD plan or continue on their current financial path.

Currently, they pay over $10,000 in interest but they get that wonderful Death Grip Interest Tax Deduction which saves them $525 in taxes. If instead, they choose to follow the IYD plan, they can eliminate their debt, and save thousands of dollars in interest each year and pay only a little more in taxes.

WHICH MAKES MORE SENSE?

Of course it makes more sense to save money on interest instead of getting the deduction. But as we already know, mortgages bring up many emotions among people. Hopefully, for the sake of your financial future, you can fight through the emotion and look at the issues objectively and logically.

We started this discussion looking at the "marginal tax benefit." As you can see, the marginal tax benefit, or the additional money you save on taxes, because of your mortgage, is much less than the cost of your mortgage interest. In our zeal to save on taxes, do we really want to spend more money than we need to on something else?

So even while it may be true, that the mortgage interest tax deduction is one of the last deductions available, you can see why…

It doesn't make financial sense to keep your mortgage just to save money on taxes!

Our typical family spends over $10,000 per year on mortgage interest. Use the table earlier in this chapter and determine how much interest you are paying with each mortgage payment. Then figure out what your marginal tax benefit is. Calculate how much you'll pay in taxes with and without the mortgage interest deduction. If you don't know how to figure this out, pay a tax person to do it. It will be worth the time or money.

You'll be surprised to learn that…

The money you pay on your mortgage interest is 10 to 20 times more money than the additional money you'll get back on your taxes!

Bottom line folks…

The mortgage interest tax deduction is one deduction you want to get rid of as soon as possible!

Let's move on to the third myth of mortgages.

MYTH # 3 – Why pay extra on your mortgage when you can do much better by investing the money in the stock market!

When you talk to people about paying off your mortgage, you'll hear that you can do better with your money! People say "put the money in the market!" Of course, most of the people who say this are stockbrokers!

Let's look at the logic. If you pay off your mortgage, aren't you getting the same return as whatever the interest rate? For example, our typical family has a 7.11% mortgage rate. If they pay off their mortgage, they get a 7.11% return on their money.

If someone invests in the stock market, what kind of a return are they going to get? Some will say you could have gotten a return of 30, 40, 50% or more during the last half of the 1990s. Others will say since you have no idea how the stock market will do, you should use the long-term average. Since the stock market crash of 1929, the stock market has averaged about a 10% return.

Let's assume these numbers are correct – paying off your mortgage earns you 7.11% and the stock market pays you 10%.

Based on these numbers, wouldn't it make sense to put any extra money you have into the stock market? I mean, you are earning about 3% more interest! It's not necessarily that simple.

When making investment decisions, there are two primary investment characteristics that people consider. They are often referred to as "Risk & Return." Return refers to "how much money can I make?" On some investments, return is interest or dividends. On stock, return can also include growth. Growth is when a stock goes up in price. Risk refers to the safety of the investment. Is it very speculative (which usually has the highest potential for growth) or is it very safe (some investments are guaranteed).

There is typically a direct relationship between risk and rate of return. They tend to move in the same direction. The higher the risk is, the higher the rate of return will be. The lower the risk is, the lower the rate of return will be. For example, very safe investments (low risk) tend to not make much money (low return) but you can count on them. Speculative (high risk) investments can make lots of money (high return), but you could lose all your money as well.

When choosing between investing in your mortgage or investing in the stock market, these two investment characteristics are important. Look at the following table:

	Invest in your Mortgage	Invest in the Stock Market
Tax Free Return? (Return)	YES	NO
Guaranteed Return? (Risk)	YES	NO

If you want to analyze your return, you should always look at the tax ramifications. How would this investment affect your taxes, especially if you make money on the investment? The tax impact will affect your return.

When you invest in stocks, the stocks grow in value over time. Let's say your stocks double in value over 10 years. You paid $5000 for some stock and you sell them for $10,000. The gain is the difference between what you paid for the stocks and what you were paid when you sold them. When you sell the stock you are taxed on the gain of $5000. You will pay capital gains tax on this gain. The tax could be as much as your ordinary income tax rate or it could be less depending on a number of factors.

Now some people will argue, "What if I invest in my 401(k) or my IRA instead of investing in my mortgage? My gains are tax-free!"

We need to make a distinction between **tax-free** and **tax-deferred**. Tax-free means you pay no taxes on growth or gain. There are not many tax-free investments other than municipal bonds. Tax-deferred means you pay taxes later. Typically taxes are paid when you withdraw money from the investment. For the purpose of this discussion, we are assuming your investments are not tax-free.

When you pay off your mortgage, you do "earn" money. You do get a gain. This gain is the future payments you will not need to make. For example, let's say you have a mortgage payment of $1000 and you pay your mortgage off in 15 years instead of 30 years. Your gain is the $1000 each month that you get to keep in your pocket for the next 15 years instead of sending that $1000 to the mortgage company. By the way, if you get to keep an extra $1000 each month for 15 years, that's $180,000 you get to keep!

When you enjoy a "gain" on your investment by paying off your mortgage early, that gain has one important benefit. Any gain you receive by paying off your mortgage is tax-free! In other words, the extra thousand you get to keep in your pocket for the next 180 months is money on which you will not be taxed!

So there are definitely tax differences when comparing investing in your debt to investing in the stock market. The gains you make in the stock market will be taxed sooner or later. For the purpose of this discussion, we will assume the total tax on stock market gains is 25%.

When we factor the tax implications into our investment decision, you see a very different picture. By paying off your mortgage early, you get a 7.11% rate of return (or whatever your interest rate is). If you invest in the stock market, you will get about a 10% rate of return over the long term. But remember, that stock market growth is taxed. At a 25% tax rate, your 10% rate of return in the stock market is an **after-tax rate of return of 7.5%!**

If you look at long-term averages and consider taxation, you can see that investing in the stock market really isn't a better rate of return. Many "market experts" however will argue this point. They will say "with good research and smart investing, you can do much better than 10% in the market. Let's analyze this argument.

For some people certainly, they can get a better than 10% rate of return in the market. However, there are additional factors to consider. What is the price of this advice and research? Again, when you look at rate of return, you have to subtract taxes and broker fees to look at what your real return is.

While we don't argue the point that some people do much better than a 10% rate of return there is another aspect to consider. What is the risk of the investment?

Risk will vary with your stock market investment. Depending on whether you invest in mutual funds, bonds, options, derivatives, or whatever vehicle, risk varies. In all of these investments, however, there is one important risk…

You risk that you might lose all of the money you put into the investment!

Now we don't say this to scare people away from the stock market. Since we want to compare investing in your mortgage to investing in the stock market, we need to compare risk.

We can all agree that while the stock market has the potential for great returns, it also has the potential for great losses as well. If you got in early on the Internet stock rage, you may have had huge gains. However, if you kept your Internet stocks, you may have lost all of your gains or even all of your money. There is no doubt you can have hot streaks and cold streaks with the stock market as we have seen over the last few years. Whether your investments go up or down, we can all agree that there is an inherent financial risk when you invest in the stock market. You could do well but you could also lose all your money!

What is the financial gain when you invest in your mortgage? You gain by paying down principal – you then owe less money. You gain by eliminating future payments. In other words, when you pay down principal, you decrease the number of payments you will have to make in the future.

Could you lose the gains you make? Once you pay principal, could the mortgage company come back to you and say you need to pay it again? No way! Once your mortgage is paid off, and you are enjoying the extra money in your pocket each month, is there a risk that you might lose the gain, that you might need to start making mortgage payments again? Of course not!

So when analyzing risk between investing in the stock market and investing in your mortgage, the comparison is easy!

Investing in the stock market always has risk – INVESTING IN YOUR MORTGAGE IS ALWAYS RISK FREE!

Summary

Understand that we are not against mortgages. In fact, we agree that almost everyone needs to get a mortgage, at least when they buy their first house. What we are against is keeping a mortgage for 30 years, or even worse, keeping a mortgage forever. Most people do keep their mortgage forever because they are either moving to a new house and mortgage or refinancing their existing mortgage. And it's this situation of keeping your mortgage for 30 years or forever that that robs people of hundreds of thousands of dollars in wealth, and prevents them from achieving true financial freedom.

Now that you know how to invest in your debt, and quickly eliminate your mortgage, would you agree that you have a choice regarding your mortgage? You can either keep it or you can invest in it and eliminate it. Therefore, isn't it proper to say…

A mortgage is an optional choice, even if you want to own a home!

Considering that the typical person will pay hundreds of thousands of dollars in interest on their mortgage loan, isn't this at least a $100,000 choice? The choice is fairly simple. Do you want to give more than $100,000 in your hard-earned wealth to the mortgage company or would you prefer to keep it for yourself and your loved ones? We assume you would prefer to keep it, so go out there and *Invest in Your Debt*!

Even though you now know how and why to pay off your mortgage, the purpose of this chapter is to help insulate you from the conventional wisdom about mortgages that will be shoved in your face when you tell others about your IYD plan. There are few conventional advisors such as financial planners, CPAs, insurance agents, etc. who will encourage you to pay off your mortgage. Why would they advise against something that has such a positive impact on your financial future?

There are probably a number of reasons for this attitude from traditional advisors. First, they have been schooled in the same conventional wisdom the rest of us have been. They need to read this book and come to our class as much as anybody else because they face the same financial challenges the rest of us face. A second reason may have something to do with the incomes of traditional advisors. If you choose to first invest in your debt that means the extra money you have will be used for something other than the products traditional advisors sell. If they sell fewer products, they make less income!

Now we are not saying that traditional advisors are only concerned with their own income. But you can imagine it may be difficult for them to accept a perspective that results in fewer sales for them! Of course, if a traditional advisor looks at IYD as a "fewer sales for them" perspective, that is a very short-sighted view.

Once you have finished investing in your debt, you will need to find other investments, traditional investments. The traditional advisors could then be an important part of your journey to true financial freedom. If they encourage clients to invest in their debt, they may give up a client who can invest a hundred dollars or so a month now. But in return, they can have a client who, in a few years, is able to invest thousands of dollars each month. Now if you were a professional advisor, which type of client would you rather work with?

Scott Burns has been a popular financial advice columnist for many years. His column entitled *Your Money* is syndicated and appears in newspapers around the country. There was a time when he promoted the conventional wisdom of "Don't pay off your mortgage – invest that money instead." A few years ago, Scott Burns was exposed to the *Invest in Your Debt* concept. Now he is a big believer in the **investment value** of paying off your debt and your mortgage.

If a traditional financial advisor gives you grief about your desire to *Invest in Your Debt*, point them to Scott Burns' web site (www.scottburns.com). Mr. Burns has written a number of excellent articles on the topic of paying off your mortgage. We encourage readers of this book to visit his site as well.

Your mortgage is the biggest financial hurdle standing between you and true financial freedom. You now have a plan for overcoming this obstacle and turning your financial life around. Don't let those who are ignorant of the benefits of investing in your debt stand in your way. When the "know-it-alls" of the world tell you how stupid it is to pay off your mortgage, just smile to yourself and know they are simply reciting conventional wisdom.

Revisit this chapter to help keep you on track. Don't let the dream-stealers take your dreams away. Trust yourself and your knowledge of how to achieve true financial freedom, by first investing in your debt!

Chapter 8

Debt Freedom Leads to Financial Freedom

At some point in our lives, we've all dreamed about financial freedom. Maybe we didn't call it that…but we did think about it.

How nice would it be if all your bills were paid…
How little stress would you have if you weren't worried about job security…
How wonderful would it be to have no financial worries…

If you've ever dreamed of these things…you've dreamed of true financial freedom.

Traditionally, for most of us financial freedom has meant the same thing as wealth. You know – filthy, stinking rich – rolling in the dough. We have grown up also believing that "it takes money to make money," that to be financially free you must have a great deal of money invested. This pile of money must be so big, that it generates huge amounts of interest income.

What does conventional wisdom tell us about how you build this big pile of money? The familiar advice of "pay yourself first" and "save 10% of your income" is what most of us were taught. Conventional wisdom says if we just save some of our money, we will achieve financial freedom.

How has conventional wisdom worked for you? Have you begun saving and investing – **on a serious basis?** We're not talking about $50 or $100 per month – we're talking about saving and investing enough on a monthly basis so in the near future you will be financially free? For the typical baby boomer, this could mean needing to save about $2000 per month to achieve true financial freedom at retirement.

"$2000 per month! You've got to be kidding – there's no way I could invest $2000 each and every month." Are you investing $2000 each month? Do you even know anyone who is?

Do you even believe you can free up enough of your income from expenses to begin saving? And if you can begin saving, do you believe saving and investing will lead you to true financial freedom? Most people have lost their faith in this conventional approach.

A poll sponsored by the Consumer Federation of America, shows that less than 50% of people believe saving and investing some of their income was the most reliable route to wealth.

Because most people equate financial freedom with huge piles of wealth, is it any wonder that most families give up on becoming financially free. Most families are living payday to payday with little or no savings, and no real options to break free from the cycle. They are resigned to the fate of "getting by." They feel financial freedom is outside of their control, unless they "get lucky."

The poll sponsored by the Consumer Federation of America, also shows that 28% of people believe winning a lottery or sweepstakes is "their best chance to obtain a half a million dollars or more in their lifetime."

Now just why do people feel this way?

People believe "it takes money to make money" (e.g. investments). They just simply have no idea how they will ever be able to save and invest the amount of money needed to achieve true financial freedom.

Let's take a quick time-out to communicate a very important message:

The *Invest in Your Debt* program is YOUR best opportunity to obtain half a million, or one million, or even more dollars in your lifetime. In fact, for the typical family, IYD is the only realistic chance they have to create real wealth and to achieve true financial freedom.

The *Invest in Your Debt* program is your roadmap to true financial freedom. Financial freedom can seem so far away that it is hard to imagine it ever happening for you. But suspend your disbelief and trust the process. IYD works regardless of your current financial status! In fact, it's guaranteed to work because it is based on simple mathematical principles.

These principles boil down to some basic facts. Compound interest is the magic ingredient for creating true financial freedom. When it works for you everything is terrific. When it works against you, your financial life quickly becomes a disaster. IYD teaches you how to turn compound interest into your most important wealth-building tool instead of letting it steal your wealth from you.

An important perspective in the *Invest in Your Debt* program is that debt freedom equals financial freedom. Think about it for a moment. How many of you are making enough money? Anyone? (usually about 4% of the people in our workshops say they are making enough money). If you think you are not making enough money think about this…

IF YOU HAD NO DEBT, HOW WOULD YOU BE DOING ON YOUR CURRENT INCOME?

What would your financial life be like if you had no credit card payments, no student loan payments, no car payments, no home equity loan payments, NO MORTGAGE payment? You'd be doing pretty darn well, wouldn't you?

In this book we have laid out a practical, step-by-step method that you can follow to achieve true financial freedom. The plan is momentum-based where we make small gains in one area of our financial life, and then leverage those gains into even bigger gains until you reach the point where you are saving and investing $1000, $2000, $3000 or more EACH AND EVERY MONTH.

If you had $1000, $2000 or even more left over to save and invest each month, DO YOU THINK YOU COULD CREATE REAL WEALTH AND ACHIEVE TRUE FINANCIAL FREEDOM?

Of course you could, and that's the beauty of *Invest in Your Debt*. We show you how to…

Reach the point where you are able to save and invest a huge amount of money each and every month.

We teach you how to get to that point by…

First investing in your debt, then once your debt is eliminated redirecting the money you had been wasting on debt payments into traditional investment vehicles.

Here's the good news – YOU ALREADY HAVE ENOUGH MONEY IN YOUR LIFE TO ACHIEVE TRUE FINANCIAL FREEDOM. At least for most people, the amount of money they earn is not the problem. The amount they keep is the problem. Once you are able to keep enough, you can invest enough to quickly build a nest egg large enough to retire on.

Different people have different definitions of retirement. Our definition of retirement is simple. If you can get up in the morning (or afternoon if you like to sleep in!) and do what you want, not what some company or boss wants you to do, then you are retired!

How do you get to the position where you keep enough to create your own financial freedom? You first invest in your debt and put the power of compound interest to work for you by eliminating your debt. Right now, compound interest is working against you because it is earning money for your creditors (based on your debt) – compound interest is costing you money. If you can shift this paradigm from one where you pay compound interest on your money to one where you earn compound interest on your money, then true financial freedom is within your grasp.

Does this give you a better understanding of why we say…

Debt freedom leads to true financial freedom

Once you eliminate your debt, you are then in a position to save and invest enough money to build a nest egg you can live off of forever.

Now the cynics will say, "Yeah, but it still takes a long time to build a big enough nest egg, even when you are putting $2000 a month into investments." This is true. If we assume that it takes a $1 million nest egg to achieve financial freedom, even if you invest $2000 each month, and assume an average of 10% growth, it will take about 17 years for your nest egg to grow to a million dollars.

If you are one of the cynics, what is your current plan for achieving true financial freedom? Are you going to be able to retire when and how you want to? Or are you going to retire the way most people do – **THEY DIE BEFORE THEY RETIRE FROM THEIR JOB!**

The *Invest in Your Debt* system helps people address the largest financial concerns they typically face in their lifetimes. Can I pay off my mortgage before retirement? How will I ever be able to save for retirement? Can I afford to send my kids to college? While there are many financial advisors available to help people answer these questions, too often their advice is biased by commission-generating products the advisors sell.

If you are currently able to invest enough money each month so that you can achieve your financial dreams, then we congratulate you! If however, you are like most people, and are not on the road to true financial freedom, we hope for the sake of you and the people you love you will take action. We believe the best action you can take for your financial future is to **FIRST INVEST IN YOUR DEBT!**

Appendix A1

Appendices

Spendsmart Family Overview

Why do we call our typical family the "Spendsmart" family? Because they were smart enough to attend an *Invest in Your Debt* Class seven years and 11 months ago! Now after investing in their debt, they are debt free and are beginning to build real wealth with the money they were previously wasting on debt payments. Let's follow through the timeline of where they stared and where they end up.

Seven Years and 11 months ago...

When the Spendsmart family started following the *Invest in Your Debt* process their financial situation looked like this:

Debt	Balance	Monthly Payment	Interest Rate	Months to Pay Off
MasterCard	$972	$24	22.9	6 yr, 6 mo
Discover	$2,755	$41	9.9	8 yr, 2 mo
VISA	$4,286	$86	18.9	8 yr, 2 mo
Her Car	$8,150	$359	7.12	2 yr, 0 mo
His Car	$11,650	$308	12.60	4 yr, 0 mo
Home Equity	$31,242	$389	10.11	11 yr, 3 mo
Mortgage	$110,286	$757	7.11	28 yr, 1 mo
Totals	$169,341	$1964		

Their annual gross income is $51,188. They decide to create a 10% Spend Smart Factor so they begin investing an additional $427 in their debt.

Today...

The Spendsmart family is now debt free! Debt freedom gives them a large degree of financial freedom. Look at the before and after picture:

Monthly	7 years 11 mo ago	Today
Income:	$4,266	$4,266
Living Expenses:	$2,302	$1,875
Debt Expenses:	$1,964	$0
Total Expenses:	$4,266	$1,875
Expenses as % of Income:	100%	44%
Spend Smart Factor	$0	$427
Money Saved on Debt Payments	$0	$1964
Money Available to Invest:	$0	$1964
Interest Saved	$0	$118,525

Not only are they debt free, but they are moving quickly towards true financial freedom. Now they can live on much less income. Since their expenses no longer include debt payments, they no longer spend 100% of their income. In fact, now that they have a Spend Smart Factor and are debt free, they can live on 44% of their income because their living expenses are only $1875.

The ability to live on less income gives the Spendsmart family the opportunity to make some choices they could never had made when they were in debt. For example, they no longer need to be at the mercy of unpredictable job futures. Have you ever worried about losing your job through a merger or downsizing? If one of the Spendsmarts loses their job, it would no longer be a financial disaster because they only need about half of the income they previously needed when they were carrying their debt load. Have you ever wished you or your spouse could stay home with the children. The Spendsmart family can now have a stay-at-home parent, if that is what they choose.

What if the Spendsmart family chooses to keep their income at the same level, and they simply begin investing in traditional investments. Now that they are debt free, they have plenty of "extra" money to invest each month by using the money they were previously wasting on debt payments added to the Spend Smart Factor!

Eight Years and 5 month from today...

Just eight years and 5 months after the Spendsmarts achieve debt freedom they achieve financial freedom! They took the money they had been investing in their debt ($1964 minimum payments plus their Spendsmart factor of $427) and began investing it in traditional investments growing an average of 10% a year, once they became debt free. We refer to this as financial freedom, because the earnings on their traditional investment nest egg covers their Living Expenses.

Monthly Investment:	$2391
Rate of Return:	10%
Length of Time:	8 years, 5 months
Investment Value:	$375,000
Monthly Earnings:	$1875
Monthly Expenses:	$1875

In this example, we assume the monthly earnings give a 6% return in order to estimate the impact of taxes. Now, 16 years and four months after the Spendsmart family began to invest in their debt, they can continue to live the way they live and never worry about money again.

15 Years and one month from today...

The Spendsmarts are millionaires! They have a net worth of over $1,000,000! They took the money they had been investing in their debt ($1964 minimum payments plus their Spendsmart factor of $427) and began investing it in traditional investments growing an average of 10% a year, once they became debt free.

Monthly Investment:	$2391
Rate of Return:	10%
Length of Time:	15 years, 1 month
Investment Value:	$1,001,648

They have become millionaires by focusing on two areas of their financial life. First, they worked hard to create a Spend Smart Factor so they could

158

leverage a few hundred dollars a month into the fuel that speeds their journey to financial freedom. Second, they invested in their debt first, and once debt free they invested the money they had been wasting on debt in traditional investments.

Because the Spendsmart family is now one of the "Millionaires Next Door," they choose to live on less than they make. They have achieved TRUE FINANCIAL FREEDOM just 23 years from the day they began investing in their debt. They have TRUE financial freedom because their investments have grown so large they produce more income than the Spendsmarts could possibly spend.

Investment Value: $1,001,648
Rate of Return: 10%
Monthly Earnings: $8347
Monthly Expenses: $1875

Appendix A2

What Should I Pay First?

INITIAL SPEND SMART FACTOR: _____
(10% of Gross Income Suggested)

Name Of Debt	Starting Balance	Minimum Monthly Payment	Spend Smart Factor	Invest in Your Debt Amount	Debt Free Date Factor
TOTALS:					

How will you determine which to pay first? Decide how you want to prioritize your debt. We suggest you pay the debts in order from lowest to highest balance, though you may choose some other method of prioritization such as highest to lowest interest rate. Make sure you use minimum monthly payments only, even if you are currently paying extra money on your debt. Your mortgage payment should include only the principal and interest portions of your debt (do not include the insurance and tax portion of your payment).

The _Invest in Your Debt_ Amount is the sum of the minimum payment added to the Spend Smart Factor. When your first priority debt gets paid off, the _Invest in Your Debt_ Amount from the first debt becomes the Spend Smart Factor for your second debt. When your second priority debt gets paid off, the _Invest in Your Debt_ Amount from the second debt becomes the Spend Smart Factor, and so forth.

Typical Family Example

INITIAL SPEND SMART FACTOR: **$427**
(10% of Gross Income Suggested)

Name Of Debt	Starting Balance	Minimum Monthly Payment	Spend Smart Factor	Invest in Your Debt Amount	Debt Free Date Factor
MasterCard	$972	$24	$427	$451	2
Discover	$2,755	$41	$451	$492	6
Visa	$4,286	$86	$492	$578	7
Her Car	$8,150	$359	$578	$937	9
His Car	$11,650	$308	$937	$1245	9
Home Equity	$31,242	$389	$1245	$1634	19
Mortgage	$110,286	$757	$1634	$2391	46
TOTALS:	$169,341	$1964			98

Our typical family begins with a Spend Smart Factor of $427. They decide to prioritize their debt from smallest to largest balance. They begin to follow the *Invest in Your Debt* process and add the $427 to their MasterCard payment. They now have a total of $451 to invest in their first debt. When their MasterCard is paid off in about two months they take the $451 and use it as the Spend Smart Factor for their second priority debt, the Discover card. They add the $451 to the Discover minimum payment of $41 and begin investing a total of $492 in their debt.

The Debt Free Date Factor is calculated by dividing the Starting Balance of a debt by the *Invest in Your Debt* Amount. If you add up the Debt Free Date Factors for each debt, your total will tell you approximately how many months (or how few months!) it will take you to achieve debt freedom, by first investing in your debt.

Appendix A3

Debt Free Date Calculator

How well will the Debt Elimination Process work for you? When will you be able to achieve financial freedom by first eliminating your debt? Use the chart below to estimate your debt freedom date.

First, select the amount of debt that is closest to your total debt in the column on the left. Then move across the row to the right, until you reach the number that is closest to the amount you are going to *Invest in Your Debt* (total of your minimum monthly debt payments plus your Spend Smart Factor). Look at the top of that column and you will see approximately how long until you reach debt freedom.

	1 Year	2 Years	3 Years	4 Years	5 Years	6 Years	7 Years	8 Years	9 Years	10 Years
Total Debt										
1,000	95	47	32	25	20	18	15	14	13	12
2,000	189	94	64	49	41	35	31	28	26	24
3,000	284	141	96	74	61	53	46	42	39	36
5,000	473	235	160	124	102	88	77	71	65	61
10,000	946	469	320	247	204	176	155	141	130	121
25,000	2,365	1,174	800	618	511	440	387	353	326	304
50,000	4,730	2,347	1,600	1,236	1,021	880	773	707	651	607
75,000	7,095	3,521	2,400	1,854	1,532	1,319	1,160	1,060	977	911
100,000	9,460	4,695	3,201	2,472	2,042	1,759	1,547	1,413	1,302	1,214
125,000	11,825	5,868	4,001	3,090	2,553	2,199	1,933	1,766	1,628	1,518
150,000	14,190	7,042	4,801	3,708	3,063	2,639	2,320	2,120	1,954	1,821
175,000	16,555	8,216	5,601	4,326	3,574	3,079	2,707	2,473	2,279	2,125
200,000	18,920	9,389	6,401	4,944	4,084	3,518	3,093	2,826	2,605	2,428
250,000	23,649	11,737	8,001	6,180	5,105	4,398	3,867	3,533	3,256	3,036
300,000	28,379	14,084	9,602	7,417	6,126	5,278	4,640	4,239	3,907	3,643
400,000	37,839	18,779	12,802	9,889	8,168	7,037	6,187	5,652	5,209	4,857
500,000	47,299	23,473	16,003	12,361	10,210	8,796	7,734	7,065	6,512	6,071

The debt data on this page is drawn from the Spendsmart family, our typical family. We assume that the number of debts, type of debts and payment amounts are proportionate to our typical family, regardless of the total amount of debt. Debt Freedom Dates are calculated using the Debt E-Racer software.

Let's look at our typical family as an example. They would look at the $175,000 row, because that is closest to their total debt. As they move to the right in this row, they find the number that is closest to their *Invest in Your Debt* Amount (minimum payments plus Spend Smart Factor) of $2391. They find $2473 is closest to the amount of their total payment and it is located in the 8-year column. Therefore, the Spendsmart family can estimate they will be debt free in eight years.

For those who would like to be more precise, you can add different rows together to have a more accurate picture. For example, let's say your total debt is $110,000. Since there is not a row for $110,000 you can add the $10,000 and $100,000 row together. What we mean is, take the number in each column of the $10,000 row and add it to the number in the corresponding column of the $100,000 row. Here are the numbers for the $10,000 and $100,000 row:

10,000	946	469	320	247	204	176	155	141	130	121

100,000	9460	4695	3201	2472	2042	1759	1547	1413	1302	1214

Adding them together, you end up with a row for $110,000 as shown below…

	1 year	2 yrs	3 yrs	4 yrs	5 yrs	6 yrs	7 yrs	8 yrs	9 yrs	10 yrs
110,000	10406	5164	3521	2719	2246	1935	1702	1554	1432	1335

Now that you have a row with a total debt amount closer to your total debt figure, you can more accurately estimate your debt freedom date. Again, move to the right in the row with your total debt. When you find the number closest to your total monthly debt payment, look to the top of that row and see how soon you can be out of debt using the IYD process.

A couple of notes for estimating. If you use a total debt figure or total debt payment amount on the chart that is more than your actual amounts, your debt freedom date will actually occur a little sooner than the chart says. If you use a total debt figure or total debt payment amount on the chart that is less than your actual amounts, your debt freedom date will actually occur a little later than the chart says.

Appendix A4

When Will I be a Millionaire?

When you apply the *Invest in your Debt* process in your life, you have the opportunity to achieve financial milestones you probably never dreamed possible. One of the milestones you can achieve is reaching millionaire status. Yes, by following IYD, YOU CAN BECOME A MILLIONAIRE!

To answer the question, "When Will I be a Millionaire," simply find the *Invest In Your Debt* Amount that is closest to the total monthly amount you invest in your debt. This is the amount you will then have available to put into traditional investments on a monthly basis when your debt is eliminated.

The Millionaire Date is the number of years and months it will take you, once you have eliminated your debt, to build $1,000,000 in real wealth by simply investing your *Invest In Your Debt* Amount money into a traditional investment that grows at 10%.

Invest In Your Debt Amount	Millionaire Date	5 Years	10 Years	15 Years	20 Years	25 Years	30 Years
500	28 years, 11 months	38,719	102,422	207,235	379,684	663,417	1,130,244
750	25 years, 1 month	58,078	153,634	310,853	569,527	995,125	1,695,366
1,000	22 years, 6 months	77,437	204,845	414,470	759,369	1,326,833	2,260,488
1,250	20 years, 6 months	96,796	256,056	518,088	949,211	1,658,542	2,825,610
1,500	18 years, 11 months	116,156	307,267	621,706	1,139,053	1,990,250	3,390,732
1,750	17 years, 8 months	135,515	358,479	725,323	1,328,895	2,321,958	3,955,854
2,000	16 years, 6 months	154,874	409,690	828,941	1,518,738	2,653,667	4,520,976
2,250	15 years, 7 months	174,233	460,901	932,558	1,708,580	2,985,375	5,086,098
2,500	14 years, 9 months	193,593	512,112	1,036,176	1,898,422	3,317,084	5,651,220
2,750	14 years, 0 months	212,952	563,324	1,139,793	2,088,264	3,648,792	6,216,342
3,000	13 years, 5 months	232,311	614,535	1,243,411	2,278,107	3,980,500	6,781,464
3,250	12 years, 10 months	251,670	665,746	1,347,029	2,467,949	4,312,209	7,346,586
3,500	12 years, 3 months	271,030	716,957	1,450,646	2,657,791	4,643,917	7,911,708
3,750	11 years, 9 months	290,389	768,169	1,554,264	2,847,633	4,975,625	8,476,830
4,000	11 years, 4 months	309,748	819,380	1,657,881	3,037,475	5,307,334	9,041,952
4,250	10 years, 11 months	329,108	870,591	1,761,499	3,227,318	5,639,042	9,607,074
4,500	10 years, 7 months	348,467	921,802	1,865,117	3,417,160	5,970,750	10,172,196
4,750	10 years, 3 months	367,826	973,014	1,968,734	3,607,002	6,302,459	10,737,318
5,000	9 years, 11 months	387,185	1,024,225	2,072,352	3,796,844	6,634,167	11,302,440

Appendix A5

Spend Smart Factor Power

With *Invest in Your Debt*, you have choices. One of the choices you have is how much extra money or Spend Smart Factor you can find to add to your minimum monthly payments. The *Invest in Your Debt* process works regardless of the size of your Spend Smart Factor. You can achieve true financial freedom, whether your Spend Smart Factor is 0% or 10%, by first investing in your debt.

Of course, choices have consequences. These consequences are not necessarily good or bad, but when you make choices it is good to make sure you understand the impact they may have. The size of your Spend Smart Factor impacts two significant aspects of your IYD plan: How long it takes to reach debt freedom, and the amount of wealth you can build.

Let's take a look at how different Spend Smart Factors affect the Spendsmarts, our typical family.

Spend Smart Factor	0%
Dollar Amount	$0
Debt Freedom Date	10 years 8 months
Millionaire Date	16 years 8 months
Wealth	$1,099,638

Spend Smart Factor	10%
Dollar Amount	$427
Debt Freedom Date	7 years 11 month
Millionaire Date	15 years 1 months
Wealth	$1,850,840

Spend Smart Factor	5%
Dollar Amount	$214
Debt Freedom Date	9 years 1 month
Millionaire Date	15 years 10 months
Wealth	$1,472,362

Spend Smart Factor	20%
Dollar Amount	$854
Debt Freedom Date	6 years 5 months
Millionaire Date	13 years 10 months
Wealth	$2,587,303

How much of a Spend Smart Factor can you create? Let these examples motivate you to discover how much faster you can achieve true financial freedom as you find ways to increase your Spend Smart Factor.

Appendix A6

How To Find Spend Smart Factor Money

There are a number of good ways to find money for your Spend Smart Factor. One of the best methods is to just simply review your current spending. Many of us are creatures of habit. We do things because "we've always done it that way!" By themselves, small changes in spending usually do not create large changes in financial results.

But when you follow the *Invest in Your Debt* program, suddenly small changes are leveraged into large results. By reviewing your spending in general areas, you have the opportunity to make small choices about spending that can produces large results in your financial future!

Use the form on the following two pages. Write down your current spending for each spending item in the "Old Choice" column. The total for this column should be close to your take home pay. If it is not, add some more categories to account for other types of spending you have not already listed. Write down your new choice, or spending amount, if you decide to choose to spend less on a spending item. The difference between your old choices and new choices is your Spend Smart Factor!

Spending Item	Old Choice	New Choice	Spend Smart Factor
Cable TV			
Car – Gas			
Car - Maintenance			
Car – Parking			
Car Insurance			
Cell Phone			
Child Care			
Clothing - Purchase			
Clothing - Cleaning			
Coffee Shops			
Convenience Stores			
Electricity			
Entertainment			
Fast Food – Breakfast			
Fast Food - Lunch			
Fast Food – Dinner			
Garbage Service			
Gas – Home heating			
Golf			
Groceries			
Hair Care			
Health Club			
Health Insurance			
Indulgence			
Internet Service			

Spending Item	Old Choice	New Choice	Spend Smart Factor
Laundry Service			
Lawn Service			
Life Insurance			
Maid Service			
Miscellaneous			
Other			
Pager			
Pet Care			
Pet Food			
Restaurants – Work			
Restaurants - Family			
Savings			
Status			
Telephone			
Travel			
Vending Machines			
Voice Mail			
Water/Sewer			
Totals	$	$	$

Appendix A7

Invest in What?

The concept of investing in your debt flies in the face of conventional wisdom, which promotes traditional investments. Our typical family starts their road to financial freedom by investing their $427 Spend Smart Factor in their debt. Conventional wisdom says they should invest that $427 into traditional investments. Let's compare both approaches and see which works best for the Spendsmart family.

Traditional Investments				**Invest in Your Debt**			
Year	Cash Fund	Stock Fund	Monthly $ Invested	Year	Cash Fund	Stock Fund	Monthly $ Invested
1	5,267		427	1			427
2	10,859		427	2			427
3	16,797		427	3	Invest	In	427
4	23,100		427	4	Debt	For	427
5	26,758	3,065	427	5	7 years	11 months	427
6	28,408	8,751	427	6			427
7	30,161	15,033	427	7			427
8	32,021	21,973	427	8	2,391		427/2391
9	33,996	29,639	427	9	14,527	17,161	2391
10	36,996	38,108	427	10	20,803	49,003	2391
15	48,683	95,765	427	15	28,060	265,776	2391
20	65,667	190,629	427	20	37,849	622,436	2391
25	88,574	346,709	427	25	51,053	1,209,252	2391
28y, 1m	106,525	489,739	427	28 yr 1mo	61,399	1,747,001	2391

Total   Wealth   **$596,264**   Total   Wealth   **$1,808,400**

In both cases, our Spendsmart family has annual income of $51,188 and the same living expenses. They choose to "pay themselves first" and invest 10% of their income. The difference is where they choose to invest this 10%, after they build a cash cushion equal to six months of expenses. Our time frame is 28 years and one month, the time it would normally take to pay off the mortgage. Let's look at both strategies in detail.

Traditional Investment Strategy

The traditional approach has our typical family investing $427 each month. First, they invest into a money market fund growing at 6%. The purpose is to build a six-month cash cushion. Since their monthly expenses are $4266, they need a "safety net" of $25,840. It takes them 53 months to build the safety net. Then they begin to invest the $427 each month in a mutual fund growing at 10% for the next 284 months, until the time their mortgage is paid off.

Following the traditional investment strategy, the Spendsmarts build wealth of $596,264 in 28 years and one month.

Invest in Your Debt Strategy

The *Invest in Your Debt* strategy also has our typical family invest $427 each month. However, they first invest in their debt. When their debt is eliminated in seven years and 11 months, they now have $1964 extra money each month since they no longer have debt payments. They add this to the $427 and begin investing a total of $2391 into traditional investments. Next they invest the $2391 into a money market fund growing at 6%. Their monthly expenses are only $2302 since they no longer have debt payments. Therefore, they only need a "safety net" of $13,812. It takes just six months to build the safety net. Then they begin to invest the $2391 in a mutual fund growing at 10% for the next 236 months, until the date when their mortgage is paid off in the traditional way.

Following the *Invest in Your Debt* strategy, the Spendsmarts build wealth of $1,808,400 in 28 years and one month.

The Mortgage Interest Tax Deduction Myth

The mortgage interest tax deduction is a great example of how conventional wisdom can get out of hand, especially when people don't really think things through and blindly follow such advice. Even worse, often in classes, we will hear stories about people whose tax advisors have told them to buy a bigger house **just so they can get a bigger tax deduction!** From solely a tax perspective it might be the right answer, but from a real wealth-building point of view it is devastating advice!

Let's look at the Spendsmarts, our typical family. How much is the mortgage interest tax deduction really worth to them?

Based on IRS tax tables	With Mortgage Interest Tax Deduction	Without Mortgage Interest Tax Deduction
Income	$51,181	$51,181
Personal Exemption	-$11,000	-$11,000
Mortgage Interest Deduction	-$10,684	$0
Standard Deduction	$0	-$7200
Adjusted Gross Income	$29,497	$32,981
Federal Income Tax Due	$4,421	$4,946
Tax Savings/Cost	$525	-$525

$525!!!!!!

For our typical family, that wonderful mortgage tax deduction saves them $525 in taxes! If this is the biggest tax deduction we have left, then it doesn't seem like it's worth getting excited about. This $525 in tax savings is the reason some tax advisors tell their clients to buy a larger house. The $525 in tax savings is the justification for millions of home equity loans.

The bottom lines is this folks…

Our typical family spends $10,684 in interest in order to save $525 on their taxes!

Now does that really make any sense? Follow the IYD plan and pay your mortgage off early. During the time you still have your mortgage, of course you should take the deduction. But pay your mortgage off as quickly as possible because…

You are much better off saving thousands of dollars on interest than saving a few hundred dollars on taxes.

Appendix A9

When Compound Interest Works For You

Einstein told us that compound interest was the most amazing invention he had ever seen. What is most amazing about compound interest is that it creates wealth. Day and night, year after year it never takes a vacation. It keeps growing and going.

Because of its power, we need to be very careful with compound interest in our lives. It is a terrific tool when it is creating wealth for you. But it can also destroy your financial future when it is creating wealth for your creditors. By following the *Invest in Your Debt* process, you can turn compound interest from a wealth-draining plague into the vehicle that takes you to true financial freedom.

The table below shows how compound interest will build wealth for you, instead of you creditors. The table assumes interest compounded monthly at a 10% growth rate and a consistent monthly investment.

Monthly Investment	5 Years	10 Years	15 Years	20 Years	25 Years	30 Years
100	7,744	20,484	41,447	75,937	132,683	226,049
200	15,487	40,969	82,894	151,874	265,367	452,098
300	23,231	61,453	124,341	227,811	398,050	678,146
500	38,719	102,422	207,235	379,684	663,417	1,130,244
750	58,078	153,634	310,853	569,527	995,125	1,695,366
1000	77,437	204,845	414,470	759,369	1,326,833	2,260,488
1250	96,796	256,056	518,088	949,211	1,658,542	2,825,610
1500	116,156	307,267	621,706	1,139,053	1,990,250	3,390,732
1750	135,515	358,479	725,323	1,328,895	2,321,958	3,955,854
2000	154,874	409,690	828,941	1,518,738	2,653,667	4,520,976
2500	193,593	512,112	1,036,176	1,898,422	3,317,084	5,651,220
3000	232,311	614,535	1,243,411	2,278,107	3,980,500	6,781,464
3500	271,030	716,957	1,450,646	2,657,791	4,643,917	7,911,708
4000	309,748	819,380	1,657,881	3,037,475	5,307,334	9,041,952
4500	348,467	921,802	1,865,117	3,417,160	5,970,750	10,172,196
5000	387,185	1,024,225	2,072,352	3,796,844	6,634,167	11,302,440

Appendix A10

Where is Debt in Your Life?

Beginning the journey to true financial freedom often requires taking a hard look in the mirror. Until someone accepts the fact that their current habits are not helping them financially, it is impossible to move ahead with the *Invest in Your Debt* strategy.

The following questions help provide a reality check. These questions are not meant to be judgmental. They are simply intended to help you objectively assess how involved debt is in your life. When you answer these questions and take honest stock of your current situation, you take the first step towards true financial freedom.

1. **Prior to coming to this class, did you know the total money you owe?**

2. **Do you use credit cards to get the mileage or other bonuses?**

3. **Do you ever use credit cards for household expenses (groceries, etc)?**

4. **Have you paid bills late or skipped payments?**

5. **Have you taken cash advances on credit cards to pay other bills?**

6. **Do you have any credit cards that are at their limit?**

7. **Do you argue often about money with your spouse?**

8. **Do you ever make minimum payments only?**

9. **Have you refinanced your mortgage in the last 3 years?**

10. **Have you ever gotten a debt consolidation loan?**

Appendix A11

Like an Unwanted Houseguest

When people write their mortgage payment check each month, they probably assume they are paying some interest. When people learn the "Rest of the Story" about mortgage interest it is quite a shock. The typical mortgage holder pays as much as twice the amount in interest as they pay in principal. Mortgage interest is like an unwanted houseguest because it never seems to go away!

People tend to get caught up in interest rates. Their main worry is "how low of a rate can I get." While it certainly is true that a lower interest rate will cost less in interest than a higher interest rate, this focus on rate completely misses the important issue about mortgage interest. The most important aspect of mortgage interest is not the percentage or interest rate – it is the total amount of money spent on interest. Which aspect of mortgage interest impacts your checkbook the most? The number of dollars you spend on mortgage interest each month, or the interest rate?

Our typical family has a 7.11% mortgage. That seems fairly low, doesn't it? But when you learn that for every dollar they send to the mortgage company, 58 cents goes to pay interest, 7.11% doesn't seem so low anymore, does it? Mortgages are interesting financial animals because they use amortization. The nature of amortization is such that interest is front-loaded. This means that your payments made earlier in the mortgage contain a much larger amount of interest than payments made later.

How Much of Your Mortgage Payment is Interest?

Interest Rate	Number of Years Paid					
	0	5	10	15	20	25
6	83 %	78 %	70 %	59 %	45 %	26 %
7	88 %	83 %	75 %	65 %	50 %	29 %
8	91 %	86 %	80 %	70 %	55 %	33 %
9	93 %	89 %	83 %	74 %	59 %	36 %
10	95 %	92 %	86 %	78 %	63 %	39 %

Appendix A12

Success Story

Those of us associated with the IYD Inc. have been teaching *Invest in Your Debt* and it's predecessors for many years. One of the greatest rewards we get is to hear from people whose lives have been improved because of the *Invest in Your Debt* program. In this section, we would like to share a few stories from people who have changed their lives and their financial futures, by first investing in their debt. For privacy sake, names in these articles are abbreviated, but the stories and the people are real.

Once people learn the *Invest in Your Debt* program, it always seems to be a great idea. Because we are human however, it can be difficult to take that first step, to take action, even when we hear a great idea. Our purpose in providing these stories is to help inspire others. Maybe you'll read someone's story and think "that sounds just like me."

When people see that someone like them has accomplished something they want to achieve, that can provide the motivation to take action. If you or someone you know, has a story about IYD and debt elimination, that might inspire others, please contact IYD. Help us on our mission to teach people how to achieve true financial freedom by first investing in their debt!

From Financial Illiteracy to Financial Freedom

Aimee K tells us a compelling story that highlights how we can make good choices in our lives, even if we have bad role models. When Aimee was growing up, her parents, her financial role models, were very much typical Americans. They lived an upper middle-class life in Westchester County, north of New York City, a place with one of the highest average levels of income in the country.

Most of us assume that people with high incomes are financially successful, financially smart. Aimee's father was a bank vice president, so it isn't surprising that the family followed conventional financial wisdom. That wisdom includes never paying off the mortgage and living a high consumption life-style using credit cards. This is the way most Americans live. So how did things turn out for Aimee's parents at retirement? Let's let Aimee tell her story…

"Five years ago, I was financially illiterate. My parents had just reached retirement age, and for the first time in my life I started to think about what I would do at retirement. I took a good hard look at my parents, and it scared me. They had wasted every penny they ever earned and then some all their lives. Now, my dad was unable to find gainful employment, and my mom, physically unable to continue working, are living a miserable retirement. They have been divorced for over twenty years, and are now forced to live together again just to make ends meet, as neither can afford to support their own household. The day I heard them discussing how **expensive** the TV Guide is, I knew I had to make some changes in my life."

"At the time, I was 32 years old, and like many people of my generation, I had gotten a good education, but had been taught no practical financial skills for living. Thankfully, I have always had a thirst for learning, and like so many things before, I decided to learn about financial planning. My first step was to study the local Continuing Education Catalog to see what was available. I signed up for a few different financial planning classes that sounded like they could help me. I can't remember a word that was said in most of the classes and I could barely stay awake through them, they were so boring. In the end, most of the teachers were usually just pitching to let them invest for me and rack up big commissions. I wasn't hoping for much more than that when I finally wandered into Dave Ireland's class, Debt Free and Prosperous Living Seminar."

"Was I in for the shock of my life! I was riveted! Not only was Dave Ireland's seminar both interesting and fun, I could feel in my gut that he was speaking the truth! Everything he said made perfect sense. Deep down I always knew that debt was bad, that mortgages should be paid off early, that I shouldn't waste money on credit card debt and high interest rates. I felt like I had found my religion. My parents had always lived high on the hog, keeping up with the Joneses, and now they lived in a rented apartment and leased their cars. Now in retirement, their lives have changed dramatically."

"On their meager social security checks and a small pension my Dad receives, they are in real trouble. If they stay healthy and live long enough, I expect that eventually their rent payment will increase to the point they can no longer afford to support themselves. That is not how I want to spend my golden years! If only Mom and Dad had been educated on how to live Debt Free before they retired, they would be very comfortable right now, instead of complaining about how expensive the TV Guide is!"

"I immediately implemented Dave Ireland's debt elimination program, and eliminated all my debts within three years. I now own, free and clear, my own gorgeous 2,356 square foot home, complete with pool & spa, a 1996 Jeep Grand Cherokee (that I purchased used, with cash) and my life! Since I was no longer wasting money on debt payments, I have had money to invest in the stock market for long term growth and a rental property I own. I plan to retire this year, quite comfortably, at age 37, with no bills except a little gas in my jeep, auto insurance, and some groceries and utilities. I take vacations when I want – with no mortgage or car payment, I never have to save for a vacation. I can afford nice clothes and entertainment. I have true financial freedom – all thanks to the education Dave Ireland gave me five years ago in his three-hour seminar, Debt Free & Prosperous Living."

WOW – What a story! Why can't you do what Aimee has done? Yes, Aimee is an exceptional person, but her financial success is based on the choices she has made, much more than who she is. She offers the following advice to people who want to achieve financial freedom by first eliminating their debt:

"The biggest thing people need to do is to change their thinking. When people think about getting out of debt, they think they will be depriving themselves. Some of my friends have accused me of being cheap. But I don't look at myself as being deprived because I didn't buy a bunch of "stuff" on credit. Instead I bought myself an early retirement. If you ever want the freedom to retire, or to quit a job you hate and find a job you love, regardless of what you can make, you need to change your thinking about debt."

Testimonial 2

Almost time to party ! Just had to tell you this....

Just this month I paid off my school loan of $10K, one and a half years ahead of schedule and paid off the siding for the house ($7K) in 12 months (not 60).

When Janet and I attended your workshop three years ago at EASTFIELD - we had 12 monthly installment payments. We paid a little extra on each monthly but still had them all.

AS OF THIS WEEK WE HAVE THREE - the house, the car and new flooring which was just put down last month and is interest free for 12 months (it will be paid off in four months) plus we purchased a camping trailer ($6K) and paid it off in less than 12 months.

I just refinanced the car - got 5.2% interest instead of 7.9% - for 36 months - when we had 40 months on the original note. I will save off the top over $1500 in interest by refinancing - and then I will save more because we will have it paid off in less than 18 months. Refinanced my house last spring - save over $4,000 initially – financed for 15 years lower interest - the prior note had 18 yrs on it. Will have the house paid off in 5 years.

We eliminated the escrow account on our mortgage payment and do our own monthly savings deposit toward the taxes and insurance (this is a NO TOUCH savings) Went from monthly car insurance payments ($7.50 per month service charge) to annual payment (with discount). Also we went from no monthly savings to over $500 a month in a saving nest egg.

THIS IS ALL THANKS TO YOU AND YOUR WORKSHOP - SETTING US ON THE CORRECT PATH!

Thanks
Joe and Janet

We have not stopped living. We go out three and four nights a week to eat. Go camping all the time. And pay cash for what we want - when we want.

We do not do without! Besides this we are looking for a piece of land to plan a retirement house on....

Testimonial 3

I bought the "*Invest in your Debt*" book at the seminar and showed it to my husband, and he has been reading it every night since I brought it home. I also went through the workbook and did my 2 credit cards with the roll-up method and even without getting a second job, I will have the 2 of them paid off in less than 2 years. My husband and I don't usually do our money together. We have been together for 14 years, but we just got married 3+ years ago, so we had our own lives, (so to speak) but this gave us an opportunity to talk about our future, money, and what we wanted to do with all of it. He is 52 and will be retiring in a few years. I am only (almost) 40 and have a long way to go before I even think about retiring, so this really gave us an opportunity to see where we are and where we want to go with our lives. I feel like God put this program in front of me to help me get on track. Thank you for a wonderful seminar. It was the best one I have been too. Keep up the good work, there are a lot of people out there like me that need this kind of help and teaching. I know a lot of them are at the school where I work. I don't know how the school system works as far as getting people in to speak, but if God wants you there, you will be. Again, thank you. You have helped to put me back on track. I'll keep you posted on our progress.
Diane

Appendix A13

Get a 37.13% Rate of Return – Guaranteed!

The title of this book refers to a 37.13% rate of return by investing in your debt. That is such a high number that most people find it difficult to believe. But it gets even more incredible. Not only do you get a large rate of return, this return is GUARANTEED RISK-FREE and TAX-FREE!

If you really can get a 37.13% rate of return, why would you not consider this as an investment option? If this rate of return is guaranteed, why would you not do everything you can to invest in your debt to your maximum ability? If this rate of return is tax-free, that makes it even more valuable. In this appendix, we will show you how we arrive at the 37.13% rate of return number so you can see it is real!

This rate of return is figured based upon the Spendsmart family's numbers. Investing in their debt creates a real difference in their financial situation. Once their debt is eliminated, they have extra money in their life. This is the money they were previously wasting on debt payments. Let's look at their monthly cash flow situation, before and after they invest in their debt.

Monthly Item	With Debt	Debt Free
Income:	$4,266	$4,266
Living Expenses:	$2,302	$1,875
Debt Expenses:	$1,964	$0
Total Expenses:	$4,266	$1,875
Spend Smart Factor	$0	$427
Money Saved on Debt Payments	$0	$1964

By investing their $427 Spend Smart Factor in their debt, they are debt free in seven years and 11 months (95 months). Our typical family will have an extra $1964 each month each and every month flowing through their life because that $1964 is no longer hijacked by debt payments. So the return in terms of dollars is $1964 each month.

What other options does the Spendsmart family have to earn an extra $1964 each month? What if, instead of investing in their debt, our typical family chose to take the $427 each month and invest it in traditional investments and get extra money from investment earnings? How much of a nest egg would they need to create so it would be big enough to give you an extra $1964 each month in investment earnings?

If we assume the nest egg will produce income at a rate of 10% each year, the nest needs to grow to $235,680.

Nest Egg	Earnings rate	Annual Earnings	Monthly Earnings
$235,680	10%	$23,568	$1964

To achieve the same rate of return as investing in your debt, the $427 Spend Smart Factor needs to grow to $235,680 in 95 months. What rate of return would allow the $427 to grow that much, that quickly?

The $427 needs to grow at a rate of 37.13% to build a nest egg of $235,680 in just 95 months. You need a nest egg of $235,680 earning 10% to create an extra $1964 each month.

So you could invest in your debt and get a return equivalent to this 37.13%. Could you find a traditional investment that earns 37.13%? If you are a very experienced (and very lucky) investor, you might on rare occasions see a high return like this. But there is one very important difference between investing in your debt and investing in traditional vehicles.

Investing in your debt is guaranteed, unlike the stock market!

Even if you do get lucky and get a high rate of return on your traditional investment, there is another obstacle to face. When traditional investments grow, they are usually taxable. We recognize that there are tax-deferred investments, but you eventually have to pay income tax on investment growth. Investing in your debt, however, is not taxable (at least not yet).

Even though *Invest in your Debt* puts extra money in your pocket, these "earnings" are tax-free!

Appendix A14

Where to Invest After You Have No Debt

Investing is not and should not be a complicated endeavor.

Peter Lynch, the well-known 1980's mutual fund manager, Magellan to be exact, said that we should be investing in thing that are close to us and thing that we understand well. We understand our debt well and that should be the first thing in which we invest. When the debt opportunity is eliminated, then what? Where do we invest after that?

One of the great things about investing in your debt is the fact that you will already be investing in real estate as you pay off your mortgage. Generally speaking, real estate has proven to be a good investment, especially when it is also the roof over your head. If you have not already purchased the roof over your head, I highly recommend that that be the next major investment that you focus on. Forget about pork bellies, oil wells, Enron or any other risky investments until you own your home.

As a matter of fact, I recommend that you buy a home as soon as possible, even before you become debt free from your other obligations. In other words, if you are renting and you have car payments, credit cards and other debts, it is not necessary to eliminate all your debts before you buy a house. Remember the IYD philosophy does not believe that debt is bad or good, it just is!

The IYD Linear Math, Variable Path Process is a debt elimination process, not a debt prevention procedure.

Our objective is to show you how to eliminate debt, not to prevent you from getting debt. We do not want to stop you from getting a house because we think mortgages are bad; Just the contrary. Stop wasting money on rent and start building equity by getting a mortgage. However, don't let it hang around for 30 or 40 years or a lifetime. Use the IYD strategy to pay off the mortgage and all your other debts in one simple process that you learned in the earlier chapters of this book.

However, once you do have all your liabilities satisfied, then where do you turn? Bonds, CDs, stocks, gold, silver, more real estate, commodities, tax liens or your mattress.

You have many investment choices.

Due to inflation, over time, the purchasing power of the dollars in your mattress will buy less goods and you wind up losing value (read: Money). If you are too conservative and go with CDs or the mattress, inflation will reduce you wealth. However, if you speculate too much with your hard earned money you may lose some or all of your principle in deals that just don't turn out well (read: Enron, Worldcom, oil wells, futures, etc.)

You need to balance the realities of inflation with the speculative nature of investing, no matter in what you invest.

We believe that real estate and the stock market represent the best balance between these choices. Since you will already own your home when you reach this point in your investment life, we think it will be more prudent to diversify into the corporate stock and bonds at this time. Let me stop right now and reiterate that we at IYD Inc. do not sell stocks, mutual funds, bonds, insurance or any other investments. We are strictly an educational company focusing on debt elimination seminars and personal financial coaching.

However, I have been a student of the stock market since the 1960's and have experienced and seen a lot of stock market turmoil. The one thing of which I am totally convinced is the fact that <u>no one can consistently predict the direction of the markets</u> over any reasonable time frame; be it one day, one week, one month, or one year.

Nor can any one consistently pick the next Wal-Marts or Microsoft with any consistency.

However, the statistical law of large numbers does apply to the stock market. With the use of the law of large numbers (read: diversification) and a technique called dollar cost averaging, history has shown that the stock market can be a reasonably safe place to invest most of your wealth. However, because the stock market is a continuously dynamic environment, I would prefer to continue this dialog on our website. I've posted our latest, most recent and best IYD thinking on our website. Go to www.InvestinyourDebt.com to continue reading about our overall strategy to build real wealth and achieve true financial freedom after you are out of debt. This way I'm sure you will be getting the most up to date knowledge on this ever changing subject.

Appendix A15

ADE® the "401K Liability®" Plan

People often fail to achieve the financial results they desire due to poor habits, lack of discipline, emotional attachments to money & absence of financial education.

Before I tell you what the Automatic Debt E-Racer® Program is, let me first tell you what it is not. It's not Consumer Credit Counseling, Debt Settlement, Debt Management, Debt Negotiation or Debt Consolidation. It's not a consolidation loan, new mortgage or a HELOC Program or a loan of any kind. It uses our Linear Math, Critical Path process:

The ADE® Program is a very tall, sturdy three-legged stool that will help you achieve True Financial Freedom. On top of the stool is your debt; and without each of the three legs being sturdy and strong your debt will come tumbling down on you.

The Mvelope/Spend Smart Educational and Software System is leg one of your stool. It is strong and flexible and will allow you to manage your everyday spending to your advantage and not the creditors.

Leg two is the Interest Rate Reduction Process. It too is very strong, flexible and whether you have good credit or bad credit, it is ready to dramatically cut your high credit card interest rates in half.

The third leg is the strongest, most flexible; and is slightly longer than the other two legs. It is the Linear Math, Critical Path Methodology that will totally and completely wipe out all of you debts in record time. It is powered by our proprietary, ADE® Software. This sophisticated software uses complex algorithms to prioritize your debt in an order that rapidly erases all your debts in record time while optimizing your cash flow and not the creditors. This powerful third leg is slightly longer than the other two legs, so it can gently, but firmly allow your consumer debts, car loans, students and even your 30 year mortgage to just slide off the top of the stool and into oblivion.

With the ADE® Program, IYD Inc. will manage all your liabilities (read "bills") for you. Your deb.ts will be managed in such a way that you will never need to write another check, stuff another envelope, find a stamp at the last moment and rush to the post office in order to pay a late bill.

-Is keeping up with stressful day to day activities distracting?
-Is life's little challenges getting you off track?
-Is working a full time job and/or raising a family keeping you unfocused and undisciplined?
-Are you having trouble staying on track with your Debt Elimination Plan?
-Do you find yourself facing late payments or not following your Debt Elimination Plan at all?

If you answered yes to any of these questions the Automatic Debt E-Racer® Program is what you are looking for.

Why is ADE® so Effective?

ADE® uses a simple, but powerful, Linear Math, Critical Path process that quickly melts away all your debts. All your consumer debts, credit cards, car payments, student loans, and etc., are paid off in as little as 1 to 3 years; and then your 30 YEAR MORTGAGE is paid off in another 4 to 5 years? You truly save tens of thousands of dollars in interest costs that you are now contractually obligated to pay to your creditors. With the ADE® Program, your average Effective Interest Rate is cut in half, some as low as 2.5%. All this is done with your current income! No second job or living like a hermit in the Himalayas. Just True Financial Freedom and Peace of Mind.

The Linear Math, Critical Path process is similar to the Variable Path taught in the *Invest in Your Debt* textbook, but the Critical Path is customized to optimize ones cash flow and debt elimination time line.

If you have a 401K or similar savings plan at work, ask yourself this question; without your employer administering the plan on your behalf, would you have the discipline to save as much money from each and every paycheck as you do with the 401K? For most of us, the answer is a resounding "NO WAY!" That is precisely why we created ADE®, the " 401K Liability®" plan.

The ADE® works just like a 401K plan, except it works on your liabilities, not your assets. Just like a regular 401K, once the process is set up, it is automatic; you do not have to think about it. Someone else manages the process for you, providing the structure and discipline needed for success. Everything happens automatically for you.

What could be better than that?

The analogy that makes the most sense to me is losing weight. The concept is easy; just burn more calories than you take in! You do that and I guarantee you will lose weight; I'll stake my life on it. Getting out of debt is the same way. Just prioritize your debts (and the highest interest rate is not the best way to pay off debt) and roll run debt into the other and I guarantee you will be debt free. However, like losing weight, it's a lot easier said than done. We are faced with offers for consolidation loans, new toys to try, new things to buy. Like losing weight, the marketers are constantly bombarding us with new "Twinkies", new restaurants to visit, and etc. Thus, it is almost impossible for us to lose weight or get out of debt. However, if someone had a program that would do all the exercising for you, and eat all the right foods for you, but you could go on living your life as you do today, but they did all the work and you lost all the weight; now that would be awesome. Sorry, I don't have that kind of weight lose program for you. However, with respect to your debt, the ADE® Program does all that for you.

The ADE® Program will pay your bills and manage your liabilities in such a way that it optimizes your cash flow and not the creditors. You will learn to spend smarter and manage your spending with the revolutionary Mvelope System. It's similar to the very affective envelope system our grandparents used, but brought into the 21st century.

Your interest rates will be dramatically reduced; debts will be paid in the proper order and be paid on time so that you never incur another late fee, while your debt just melts away. Did you know if you have as little as 7 debts, there are 5040 different ways you can order and prioritize these debts for payoff. Our ADE® Software figures out which one of these 5040 ways is best for you. This proprietary software is 5 years in development and is very sophisticated and extremely powerful.

As a point of interest, all monies will remain in your checking account and under your control. All that IYD does is manage the process for you. You focus on what interest you most and what you are good at; raising a family, developing a career and making money, while IYD will focus on what it is good at; eliminating your debt rapidly.

A natural by-product of the ADE® Program is the fact that it also dramatically improves your credit score by insuring that your bills are never late; while your high credit card balances and your debt to income ratio are reduced.

You have 24/7/365 online access to your own private ADE® Progress Report.
At anytime during the month you can see positive results developing:
> The date each debt will be paid
> The remaining balance of each debt
> When each debt will be eliminated
> The total debt eliminated to date
> How many months before you will be debt free

You can make changes to your plan (add debts, remove debts, change amounts or change payment dates, etc.) as often as you want and free of charge.

The program is very flexible and it is available in a "Do it Yourself" format.

ADE® is designed to save you money!
It costs you nothing!
Your creditors pay for the ADE® Program and they don't even realize it!

WHAT A CONCEPT!

If you would like to know more about the unique ADE® Program and/or get a private, confidential, free ADE® analysis/report to see if you qualify for the ADE® Program, just e-mail Margie at IYD@InvestinyourDebt.com, or call her at 888 913 8786

Appendix A16

Interest Rate Reduction Process

How many times have your credit card interest rates been reduced without you having to do anything? That's right, not often. Credit card companies have kept a tight lid on the secret that they can and often will reduce a consumer's interest rate based on their credit history. Good Credit or bad credit makes no difference. Here is the secret we want to share with you…..ask and you shall receive.

The Interest Rate Reduction Process is a program that allows the consumer to learn firsthand what to say to their credit card companies and how to reduce the interest rates on their consumer debts; by doing so they can reduce their monthly payments and increase their FICO score. This is done during a one-on-one mentoring session with a student. We evaluate and educate the student on what will most likely be the best options for them. Then together, we call the card companies to ask for a reduced rate on the student's credit cards.

As part of this educational process, the student learns various options to move some of the balances on their high interest credit cards to reduce their interest rates even further. The reduced interest rate lowers the monthly payment and makes it possible to speed up the amount of money that goes to the principal. Ultimately, this helps them achieve True Financial Freedom sooner.

The student also learns how to increase the limits on their credit cards. This is done to reduce the percent of actual usage, which will improve ones FICO.

Not for Profit Investor Lending Institute to Help People Find More Competitive Rates for
Personal and Small Business Loans

The Institute can help borrowers compete more effectively for lower interest rate loans with new people-to-people lending marketplace where individual borrowers and investors come together to borrow and lend money to each other without the need and hindrance of banks and without any closing costs.

Individuals and small businesses who may be seeking loans can now use the Institute to take advantage of a new internet marketplace that connects lenders and borrowers together, just like EBay connects buyer and sellers together in a competitive bidding environment.

Until now, banks and credit card companies have controlled, who can receive a loan, the interest rates people pay and who is even able to obtain credit. With the Institute, individuals have the opportunity to take control of consumer credit by dictating the terms of their own uncollateralized loan and placing it up for bid in an online auction. The Institute assists new members and helps drive down their interest rates even further because of its collective repayment history."

Borrowers who use the Institute can get even lower interest rates from lenders if they are also utilizing the Automatic Debt E-Racer® Program. This is because the lenders know that their loans will be properly managed by the ADE® Program. The character and reputation of the Institute as well as the track record of the ADE® Program give lenders more confidence their loans will be repaid on time and in full.

The institute can help people with FICO Score as low as 520. Obviously, the lower the score, the higher the cost of interest. Rates can vary from 8% for good scores to 20% or higher for people with a challenging credit history.

Interested individual lenders and investors can also participate in the Institute by making uncollateralized loans to other individuals. Lenders can search for loans that meet their specific criteria, including: 1) credit scores; 2) debt-to-income ratios; and 3) historical default rates and etc. Lenders minimize their risk by bidding on many small loans across different credit grades instead of concentrating their money in one big loan to a single individual.

If you are interested in becoming an investor or a borrower with the Institute or if you would just like to know more about this unique people to people lending approach just do the following. There are no costs or obligations to join today.

If you would like to know more about the Interest Reduction Programs, just e-mail Margie at IYD@InvestinyourDebt.com, or call her at 888 913 8786

Appendix A17

Helpful Websites

www.InvestinyourDebt.com
www.Debt-Free-in-Three.com
www.DebtstoWealth.com
http://www.VisionLearningInstitute.com
http://www.Guardianz.net
www.Coachamer.com
www.LowerMyBills.com
www.Stretcher.com
www.CoolSavings.com
www.FrugalMoms.com
www.FrugalFamilyNetwork.com
www.CarSmart.com
www.Ebay.com
www.FreeSite.com
www.TotallyFreeStuff.com
www.Firstgov.com
www.nojunkfree.com
www.fastweb.com
www.all-free-samples.com
www.ifg-inc.com

Appendix A18

Contact Information

IYD, Inc.
888-913-8786
www.InvestinyourDebt.com

DISCLAIMER

The *Invest in Your Debt* Book and materials are meant to help you save money on your debt so you can use the money for other purposes. Great amounts of research and effort have gone into compiling this information and ensuring its accuracy. While the authors utilize many of the principles and ideas set forth, please be advised there may be mistakes, both typographical and in content, so it is up to you, the student of these materials to treat this book as a source of ideas but not an unquestionable truth.

Equally important, the authors cannot anticipate every possible situation and condition where information from the *Invest in Your Debt* course could be used and therefore cannot predict all possible outcomes of using this information. It is possible in some circumstances that specific tips would not be valid or would be false.

It is therefore, the responsibility of the student or reader of this book and materials to decide whether advice from this is appropriate for the reader's use in general and specific circumstances. The reader must determine

Printed in the United States
89675LV00002B/1-66/A